What readers are saying about

gifts & talents for teenagers

"This book is a must-read for every teenager because it shows not only how to tap talent, but the countless ways these gifts can be manifested in our richly diverse world."

—JUDY BOWERS, ED.D., FORMER PRESIDENT,
AMERICAN SCHOOL COUNSELOR ASSOCIATION

"It is a sad reality that many teenagers today struggle to discover their own personal gifts and talents. Fortunately, Carol Carter has written a book that will help our teens identify and celebrate their special skills and become the leaders of tomorrow. Her straightforward, common sense approach and her uncanny ability to reach out to and connect with teens make this book the right answer to important questions."

TOM O'DELL, FORMER PRESIDENT,
SMALL BOARDING SCHOOL ASSOCIATION

"As a parent, I try to recognize and encourage my children's individuality but have been at a loss to help them see the true value of their unique gifts. This book offers the tools for teens to discover talents on their own through real life examples. The journaling and self-discovery exercises are excellent! Thanks, Carol, for sharing the secrets of self-awareness, purpose and acceptance as a path to success in life!"

—ANDREA STRAUS, PARENT OF TEENAGERS

"When I was young, my grandmother used to tell me 'You will never be more than you are right now.' I always thought that was a terrible thing to say. But one day I understood what she really meant. After I graduated with my doctoral degree, she told me 'You always were Dr. Ayaz; you just didn't know it yet.' This insightful and motivating book is the tool I wish I had had back then. Take advantage of the wisdom and knowledge it contains and find out who you already are."

—DR. SANDI AYAZ, EXECUTIVE DIRECTOR,
NATIONAL TUTORING ASSOCIATION

"Finally, a book that conveys a very important message to teens: Special gifts and talents aren't something that only celebrities possess—your unique gift resides within you! This wonderful guide will help students discover their amazing qualities and empower them to maximize the treasures they possess."

—LYNNE MONTROSE, VICE PRESIDENT,
NATIONAL SOCIETY FOR EXPERIENTIAL EDUCATION

gifts&talents

FOR TEENAGERS

DISCOVERING YOUR UNIQUE STRENGTHS

Carol Carter

LifeBound

DENVER, COLORADO

LifeBound
1530 High Street
Denver, Colorado 80218
www.lifebound.com

10 9 8 7 6 5 4 3 2

ISBN-10: 0-9742044-5-5
ISBN-13: 978-0-9742044-5-1

Printed in the United States of America.

contents

CHAPTER 1

what are gifts and talents?   1

LEARNING YOUR STRENGTHS

CHAPTER 2

who am I?   17

BECOMING SELF-AWARE

CHAPTER 3

diving deep into your gifts and talents   35

DEVELOPING EXPERTISE

CHAPTER 4

expanding   53

MATCHING YOUR GIFTS
AND TALENTS TO CAREERS

quick guide to profiles

foreword

In my 30 years as a school counselor and advocate of the profession, I have seen first-hand the daunting task that faces parents, educators, and students as they attempt to discover who they are.

At the core of each person's identity is the ultimate question, and the need to answer it: What is my purpose and passion in life? Many adults, should they have the opportunity to relive their youth, would likely do things differently. They might choose to explore the world with open eyes of wonder, rather than succumbing to the very real pressures of trying to fit in and, in the process, suppressing their originality.

Gifts & Talents for Teenagers can help you open a pathway in your hearts and minds leading to genuine self-discovery. Throughout the book, Carol Carter poses questions for you to ponder regarding your strengths and weaknesses, your likes and dislikes. This process of exploration provides the glorious opportunity to reflect on what makes you unique.

The many profile stories in this book also invite you to be inspired. You will read about the real struggles of famous—and not so famous—people, who through determination and courage, and sometimes sheer serendipity, discovered what they love to do. These stories will help you recognize that the path to self-discovery and self-expression can sometimes be a lonely one, but more important, they will help you see that help is always close at hand.

This book will lead you on an expedition to know the one person you need to know best—yourself. You'll learn that what makes you different is what makes you special, and that differences are something to celebrate, not hide. To students everywhere I say, "Enjoy the journey!"

—JUDY BOWERS, ED.D., FORMER PRESIDENT,
AMERICAN SCHOOL COUNSELOR ASSOCIATION

preface

Sioux story

The Creator gathered all of Creation and said,
"I want to hide something from the humans until they are ready for it.

"It is the realization that they create their own reality."

The eagle said, "Give it to me. I will take it to the moon."

The Creator said, "No. One day they will go there and find it."

The salmon said, "I will bury it on the bottom of the ocean."

"No. They will go there too."

The buffalo said, "I will bury it on the Great Plains."

The Creator said, "They will cut into the skin of the Earth and find it even there."

Grandmother Mole, who lives in the breast of Mother Earth, and who has physical eyes but sees with spiritual eyes, said, "Put it inside of them."

And the Creator said, "It is done."

acknowledgments

this book is the result of a talented team whose gifts came together to make this project a reality. Together, we went to great lengths to capture the numerous ways gifts and talents can be used in our richly diverse world. I want to take time to gratefully acknowledge the following people who contributed so immensely to this project.

Our reviewers, whose input allowed us to crystallize our ideas:

Cindy Dunn, Nina Dunn, Peg Ross, Jessica Buchanan, Jeanne Shumway, Annie Zdrojewski, Tameca Coleman, Teressa Redding, Jesse Walker, Susan Hooper, Britton Slagle, Sheryl Green, Andrea Straus, Emily Cox, Becky Cox, Lynne Montrose, Max Montrose, Brittany Henning, Kathryn Moberg, Katherine Straus, Kim Humphrey, Jessica Obitz, Laura Daugherty, Erika Bergstrom, Sara Fuller and Kieffer Williams.

Those who helped with the dedications:

Michelle Anderson, Sarah Bender, Louise Gubb, Gina Masland—for your willingness to transform loss into purpose in memory of your loved ones.

The Carter teenaged review team:

Quintana Carter, Carson Carter, Matt Carter, Elliot Carter—for your candor.

Our senior intern:

Marjorie Anderson, who reviewed the book and contributed to our profile stories—for your ideas and your attention to detail.

Our photography intern:
Alyssa Groleau, who captured many of the images seen in this book—for your inner eye and your willing friends.

Our junior editor and photography editor:
Sara Fuller—for your vision, guidance, and inspiration.

Our senior editor:
Cynthia Nordberg—for your patience, attention to detail, and excellent instincts about what makes each person special.

Finally, I want to thank all the students, teachers, parents, coaches, and educators who dare to be courageous in discovering, developing, and defining their own gifts and talents so they can make the world a better place. Many thanks to each of you for sharing your gifts and talents to create a book we can all celebrate. Most of all, I want to thank Cynthia for her indomitable spirit and her ability to bring out the best in all with whom she works—especially yours truly.

Carol Carter

dedication

This book is dedicated in loving memory of two amazing individuals, Ashley Anderson and Tom Masland, who passionately expressed their gifts and talents in the world.

Ashley Anderson, age 16, passed away on January 12, 2006, after a courageous battle with brain cancer. Ashley was an incredibly beautiful and talented girl who understood that the best things in life, such as love, understanding, compassion, trust, honesty and friendship, are free.

Ashley was a member of the National Honor Society, varsity volleyball and track teams, and a Student Government Senator. A gifted athlete, Ashley set high jump, triple jump, and sprinting records as a freshman and was the high jump champion in her high school region. Ashley loved the outdoors and enjoyed spending time at the beach wakeboarding and in the mountains snowboarding with her friends. Her amazing positive attitude was contagious and her smile lit up the world.

Tom Masland, 1950–2005, is best remembered for being a fabulous husband and father. He also is remembered for his passion for jazz, journalism, and joy. His sister Sarah said, "Tom had many gifts and talents. The one I treasure most was his talent for enjoying being with people just as they are. People fell in love with him and then wanted to respond out of their best selves—meeting his integrity, honesty, thoughtfulness, humor, and generosity with their own."

As a foreign news correspondent, Tom Masland often covered dangerous stories around the world, including Haiti, Africa,

and the Middle East. While reporting on civil rights unrest in Monrovia (Liberia's largest city, on the west coast of Africa) during the 1990s, he pulled three chunks of shrapnel out of his arm and dressed the wound from his own first-aid kit. In a *Newsweek* magazine article (November 7, 2005), he said with a laugh, "It was the world's cheapest Purple Heart."

In addition to brilliant reporting, Tom Masland also had a gift for playing the saxophone. During his college years, while in Paris, he practiced with the famous French musician Francois Breant. Later, Masland performed gigs at jazz clubs in and around New York City.

We honor Ashley Anderson and Tom Masland, who inspire us all to fully develop our gifts and talents.

what are gifts and talents?

"It takes courage to grow up
and turn out to be who you really are."

—E. E. CUMMINGS,
20TH CENTURY POET AND ARTIST

Gift *n.* a natural endowment, aptitude, faculty, or talent

Talent *n.* a particular and uncommon aptitude for some special work or activity

This book will help you understand all the things that make you special and unique. Throughout these pages we'll use the terms *gifts* and *talents* interchangeably. Learning about your gifts and talents is important because knowing them is one of the keys to discovering your purpose in life.

When you know your strengths and what makes you feel creative, capable, and joyful, developing your unique abilities so you can use them to the fullest becomes less of a challenge. The end result is a happier and more productive life.

making the most of this book

To make the most of this book you'll want to pay close attention to four things:

- First, every chapter contains two *profile stories* about famous people (one from the entertainment industry and one from an academic field). Each profile will be followed by questions for you to answer. The purpose of these profiles is to help you see how other people discovered their natural abilities and how they handled life's difficulties and obstacles in their quest for self-discovery.

- Second, this book contains many *self-discovery* questions. Take time to answer them. Sometimes you may have trouble coming up with a response—probably because you've never thought about that particular question before. One of the objectives of this book is to help you learn how to ask tough questions and find the answers within you. We hope to stimulate your thinking in new directions. If you get stuck on a question, try discussing it with a friend or parent or with a group of students at school.

- Third, near the end of every chapter is a *Self-Discovery Activity.* These activities help you put what you've read into practice. They encourage you to recognize and develop your gifts and talents and to learn more about something you're interested in.

- Fourth, near the beginning of every chapter you'll see *Secrets.* You'll want to look for these—they are important clues to developing your full potential. Here's the first one:

S E C R E T 1

Resist the urge to be like everyone else.

You've seen clothes with labels that read "one size fits all." While that may be true for nightshirts and baseball caps, it's not true for discovering what makes you unique. The desire to fit in can be a powerful pull in your life. It is up to you to resist the urge to be like everyone else. When you identify and develop your gifts, you're on your way to figuring out your purpose, passion, and fulfillment in life.

We are all different, and our unique abilities may take a while to surface. No worries. Part of getting to know yourself involves discovering what you're good at and what you like to do. It can take years to figure out these things, and there's no need to rush. You are a precious person, and this book is designed to help you see the scope and range of who you are as you chart your options and your course toward a **fulfilling** career and life.

Fulfilling *adj.* developing full potentialities

"It's good to be crazy and creative!"

Seventeen-year-old Max Montrose loves reptiles and has loved them since he was little. Over the years, he has collected dozens of scaly creatures, including alligators and geckos. "I've always been a naturalist. In preschool, my teacher bred corn snakes. The day I watched a baby snake hatch from an egg, I was hooked," he says. At the age of 8, Max was a budding entrepreneur, earning up to $200 a week in the summer showing his reptiles at birthday parties and other social events.

Interestingly, Max's early success emerged in part from issues that could be considered setbacks. In kindergarten, Max was diagnosed with attention deficit disorder (ADD) and dyslexia. Max credits his passion for animals with helping him learn how to study. In addition to being a keen researcher, Max is a whiz at writing and delivering speeches.

Max's father, Gary, reflects, "To get him to read, which he hated, I encouraged Max to find out everything he could about an animal he wanted, so he'd know how to take care of it. He always had to do the homework first and then present his case to us—except in the case of the emu," his dad adds with a chuckle, referring to Max's pet **emu** named Eli.

Emu *n.* a large flightless bird from Australia

"I brought Eli home when he was the size of a banana," says Max. Now the creature stands six feet tall and runs freely in his back yard. "I trained him to follow me by wearing mirrors on the backs of my legs so he would think I was a bird." Max also taught his feathered friend to sit and lie down on command. When Max comes home from school, Eli runs up to him and stomps his feet, "like he's happy to see me."

Max's mother, Lynne, encouraged Max to work as an **intern** at the local zoo, where he studied the venom of rattlesnakes and scorpions. "Parents must take an active role in helping kids explore their interests. If a kid is interested in skating, I tell them to think about how people design skate parks. How did Tony Hawk turn his passion into a multi-million-dollar business? Hobbies can often evolve into careers."

Intern *n.* an advanced student or graduate usually in a professional field (such as medicine or teaching) gaining supervised practical experience (as in a hospital or classroom)

Max's profound gift branched off into other interests. One developing passion is art, specifically sculpture and film. At the suggestion of a teacher, a local television producer approached Max about creating a new show in which he interviews teens about their gifts and talents. "I know I'm lucky to have found my passion at such a young age and to see it evolve into other areas," Max says. His message to kids and teens is this: "Don't worry if you're not smart in a particular subject. Explore everything you can and don't be afraid to be different. It's good to be crazy and creative!"

Early bloomers

Some people's gifts and talents surface very early in life. When I (your author) was little, I would occasionally go to restaurants with my family. Between ordering and eating, I would get up from the table and meet the people at the other tables. I loved talking to them and found it fun and interesting to meet other people.

When I was in sixth and seventh grade, I loved to talk on the phone, talk in class, and talk at every opportunity I had. No doubt this was an extension of my earlier fascination with meeting strangers. Often, my love for talking got me into trouble. Gradually, I learned to have the discipline to channel my enthusiasm to appropriate times.

Today, I get paid to talk to people. I am a professional author and speaker. In high school, I realized that my love of meeting new people and talking was a gift, despite the trouble I got into because of it. I worked to develop judgment and realized talking in class or interrupting the teacher were inappropriate ways to express my talents. The discipline I developed helped me to manage my strength, which I still monitor today.

Like Max Montrose, I wasn't great at taking tests, the measurement most schools use to rank students academically. The things I was really interested in didn't show up well on that scale. I had to focus a lot of energy on studying and had to work to improve my listening skills.

To stretch myself, I ran for student council, which involved giving speeches and defending my ideas in front of others. This was certainly intimidating at first, but the more I did it the more comfortable I became, and my fear melted away. I gained more confidence and developed my gift of communication even though I still struggled to get good grades and learn all I could.

Once I knew my strengths, I found it easier to work on my weaknesses. I didn't know what I wanted to do with my life until I had graduated from college, but I had faith even in the midst of not knowing. I took my first job as a book salesperson for a publishing company. I continued to work hard and was promoted until I became the vice president of a division of the company. I discovered my gifts and talents early in life—I was an "early bloomer."

Another early bloomer, John, was an industrious little kid. His sister, Barb, often broke things like lamps, trinkets, and dishes. John loved putting these things back together. In fact, nothing made him happier than reconstructing these objects and thinking about his next reconstruction adventure.

In high school, John excelled in physics, math, and science. He worked very hard in English and was also a strong communicator due to his efforts in writing and taking classes from teachers who challenged him. When John started college, he knew he wanted to be an engineer.

Today, John is a civil engineer who has had a long and rewarding career as a senior manager responsible for others in his company. His gifts and talents from childhood were early clues to the profession to which he would ultimately commit. Unlike some students who are gifted academically and rest on their laurels, John worked hard to be well-rounded, volunteering at organizations and taking part-time jobs that enhanced his people skills and ability to adjust and adapt. If John had been simply satisfied with his perfect grade point average and neglected to push himself to grow emotionally and socially, he probably wouldn't be a senior manager with his company today.

Late bloomers

Other people's talents surface later, often not until they are adults. When Cynthia started college, she chose to major in business. She believed to make a living you had to study something that would help you get the best job, even if it wasn't something you really liked.

During her summer breaks from college, she began volunteering as a camp counselor. This experience showed her that she really liked helping people. She was able to help children with their problems by listening to them and sometimes giving advice. Cynthia decided to change her major from business to education with an emphasis on social work.

When she graduated from college, Cynthia got a job at a community service organization in a poor neighborhood of Chicago. She helped develop the organization's brochures and other printed materials. From this job, she discovered a second ability: writing. Today, Cynthia continues to work with students through a company called LifeBound. She greatly enjoys combining her talent for writing with her love for education. "One of the greatest lessons I've learned is that to be happy I must be able to use my gifts and talents to the fullest."

S trengths quiz

Quizzes are one way to get your creative wheels turning about what your strengths are. There are no wrong answers to self-discovery quizzes like the one here. If you like doing each option, pick the one you like the best but make a note to yourself that you enjoy the other choice(s). Keep the possible answers in mind as you go through your daily activities in the next week.

1. Would you rather work with other people or on a computer?

2. Would you rather play a team sport like baseball or compete in an individual sport like track?

3. Do you study best alone, with one friend, or in a group?

4. If you're trying to learn something new, would you rather have someone explain it to you, read about it, or see a demonstration?

5. If you have to tell someone something unpleasant, would you rather tell them in person, or on the phone, or write them a letter?

6. Are you a morning, afternoon, evening, or night person?

7. Are you a better writer if you write by hand or type on a computer?

8. When you've had a tough day, would you rather talk to a friend or be by yourself for a while?

9. To relax, would you rather do something risky like mountain climbing or something safer like walking?

10. What are your favorite subjects in school? What subjects do you like the least?

11. Would you rather read a book or play a board game?

12. Can you sit still or do you fidget a lot?

13. Do you work best with your hands or with ideas?

14. Would you rather make music, dance to music, or just listen to music?

15. Do you like to use tools and gadgets, or would you prefer tasks that don't require them?

16. Would you rather be outside or inside?

17. Would you rather fix something or write a story?

18. Do you like to have a regular schedule, or do you prefer when you're not sure what's going to happen next?

19. Would you rather design something or build something?

20. If you were helping on a disaster rescue effort, would you rather help distribute supplies to people directly or work on a team that organizes the operation?

What is your favorite free-time activity?

Another way to discover your unique strengths is by noticing what you love to do in your free time. Here's how Zak, a middle school student from Boston, described his favorite free-time activity:

"My favorite activity or sport is baseball. I just love to be throwing a ball or hitting it as far as I can. I get a great feeling when I hit the ball and get on base. Heck, I feel great when I'm in the on-deck circle. Mentally, when I get a hit or make a play in the field, I know that I get better by practicing and trying harder every time I play. Physically, when I get a hit, I know that I have gotten stronger either by practicing or thinking about how I want to approach the pitcher. If I know that he is a curveball pitcher, I usually move up in the box. If he is a fastball pitcher, I might move back in the box so that I have maybe a second more to think if I want to swing or not. You don't have much time to decide, so every second counts."

Fifteen-year-old Alisha of Chicago loves interpretive dance. She performs for school plays and community events and wears costumes related to the theme of the events. In her free time, Alisha likes to listen to music and create her own dance moves. She also helps other dancers choreograph their routines. "When I'm dancing I feel truly free to be me," she says.

Throughout this book you'll learn many clues about how to discover your natural talents. The best way to make the most of this book is by answering the "self-discovery" questions in each chapter.

SELF-DISCOVERY QUESTIONS

Now it's your turn. In your free time, what is one of your favorite activities?

_____

_____

Describe this activity as if you were teaching it to someone who doesn't know anything about it. Give instructions and write down anything else you know about the interest or activity.

_____

_____

_____

_____

_____

What do you like about this activity? Think of as many reasons as possible for why you like it.

_____

_____

_____

_____

SHAKIRA

Shaking it up

"Shakira's music has a personal stamp that doesn't sound like anyone else's. No one can sing or dance like her, at whatever age, with such innocent sensuality, one that seems to be of her own invention." (8notes.com)

hakira Isabel Mebarak Ripoll, better known to the world as simply "Shakira," was born February 2, 1977, in Barranquilla, Colombia. Her family was very poor. Shakira's mother was Colombian and her father's family was from Lebanon. This mixed heritage allowed her to soak up music from both cultures.

Shakira has always been passionate about music. When she was nine years old, she discovered her gift for writing songs and composing music. At age 10, she tried out for her school choir but was rejected because she didn't have the typical singing voice of a young girl. Instead, her voice was low and gritty. She didn't let that deter her, however. Shakira began entering local competitions and won many of the talent contests in her hometown.

At age 13, Shakira recorded her first album for Sony Colombia, which consisted of songs she herself had written. It sold well locally but did  not gain international recognition, which was disappointing. She was even more disappointed with the pop sounds of her second album. It did not reflect the music she could hear in her mind. She became discouraged, causing her to abandon music for a while and act in a Latin soap opera.

In 1995, Shakira went back to performing music with a new attitude. This time she was determined to retain far more control over her work, a difficult feat for any artist. She worked rock and roll rhythms, along with occasional Arabic tinges, into her Latin pop material. The album started out as a slow seller but gradually climbed in popularity. Her next album did even better and cracked the American Latin billboard charts.

Then, Gloria Estefan, a Cuban-American musician, offered to help translate her music into English. This crossover into the English-speaking world launched Shakira into superstardom. In order to maintain control over her work, Shakira learned English. She now speaks five different languages: Italian, Spanish, English, Arabic, and Portuguese.

At the age of 26, Shakira became the youngest person ever to be appointed a UNICEF goodwill ambassador. As a UNICEF ambassador, Shakira travels to see first hand the struggle of millions of children in developing countries. "She uses her popularity and her personal interest in children's issues to support UNICEF's mission to ensure every child survives and thrives through adolescence" (Unicef.com).

Shakira could have left her career in the hands of those in the music industry but chose instead to go with her instincts, drawing inspiration from her rich cultural background. She had to overcome her family's lack of resources, initial disappointments, and pressure to be like every other female pop singer. What a great decision that has turned out to be.

Sources: 8 Notes: Shakira biography. www.8notes.com/biographies/shakira.asp.

Unicef.com Press Releases: *Singer and songwriter Shakira appointed UNICEF Goodwill Ambassador,* www.unicef.org/media/media_15183.html.

VH1 Artists A–Z Biography: Shakira, www.vh1.com/artists/az/shakira/bio.jhtml.

Profile Clues to Use

How did Shakira develop her abilities?

_____

_____

_____

What are some obstacles she had to overcome?

_____

_____

_____

How do you see yourself as similar or dissimilar to her?

_____

_____

_____

Other people have used their gifts and talents to tackle world-wide problems, as the following profile shows.

DAVID HO

Decoding HIV

"This [AIDS] is a problem for the world and therefore we're going to solve it."

—DAVID HO, SPEAKING ABOUT AIDS AT THE 2000
AMERICAN MEDICAL ASSOCIATION CONVENTION

David Ho was born in Taiwan in 1952. When David was three, his father moved to the United States to study engineering and make a better life for his family; David and the rest of his family were left in Taiwan. When his father sent for the family, David, age 12, did not speak English:

David spent his first months of school in frustrated bewilderment, unable to follow lessons in the unfamiliar language. He was ridiculed by his classmates for his inability to speak or understand, but within six months he had made progress in the language, and graduated with honors. (The Academy of Achievement)

Despite his difficult beginnings, David worked very hard and earned degrees from prestigious colleges and hospitals, such as Harvard Medical School and Cedars-Sinai Medical Center/UCLA School of Medicine.

David then turned his focus to AIDS research. In the early years after the human immunodeficiency virus (HIV) was identified, researchers believed that the virus was dormant and became active only after months or years. This is because people did not seem sick when they were first diagnosed. However, David did not believe that was how the virus worked. Through his research, David proved that HIV weakens the immune system right from the start, so that people with AIDS die from common diseases.

Until David's important discovery, researchers focused on the end of a person's life. David pioneered the research that caused scientists to focus on slowing HIV's destruction from the earliest stages of infection. He was essential in creating the combinations of medications that are now the standard for treatment of people with HIV. When David started his research, he had no way of knowing if he was on the right path. He only knew that people were dying and something had to be done. The same tenacity that helped him as a non-English-speaking immigrant get through school has improved the quality of life for millions with HIV and brought research much closer to a cure.

David has won many awards and holds several prestigious positions. Two of the most important awards he has won are *Time* magazine's "Man of the Year" in 1996 and a Presidential Medal in 2001. He is an international leader in the fight against the disease and heads up a consortium of Chinese and American organizations to help address the crisis of HIV/AIDS in China.

David's gifts and talents were only a part of his success. He had to be willing to work long and hard to overcome the obstacles placed in his path and to receive the education and develop the necessary skills to conduct research. David trusted his own instincts when it came to the way HIV works and was willing to devote himself to his passion. In the end, he has prolonged the lives of many and will ultimately be instrumental in finding a cure to end AIDS.

Academy of Achievement: David Ho. www.achievement.org/autodoc/printmember/hoa0bio-1.

Aaron Diamond AIDS Research Center Research Labs: David D. Ho, M.D. Brief Biography. www.adarc.org/research/ho/ho-bio.htm.

Profile Clues to Use

How did David Ho develop his abilities?

What are some obstacles he had to overcome?

How do you see yourself as similar or dissimilar to him?

"My Interests" portfolio

This portfolio can be a combination scrapbook/photo album. You can include all kinds of things here: pictures, drawings, magazine and newspaper articles, brochures, tickets, postcards, certificates, ribbons won, almost anything! The idea is for the collection of items to showcase your uniqueness. Make a list of items that you could place in your portfolio:

_____

_____

_____

_____

Next, read an article from a trustworthy publication or research a person or topic you're interested in. Write to that publication asking for more information about this particular person or subject. Create a file folder (an actual folder or one on the computer) and begin saving magazine articles, newspaper clippings, or anything you've done yourself that relates to your interests.

For example, let's say you're interested in learning more about nature. You could visit a nearby zoo, museum, and/or a college campus and ask for any printed information they have related to nature. During the summer, you could volunteer for the nature center at a summer camp. You could interview the person in charge, write it up in a question/answer format, and add this to your folder. Over time you'll have accumulated valuable information about your hobby or interest.

2

who am I?

"No price is too high to pay
for the privilege of owning yourself."

—FRIEDRICH NIETZSCHE

S E C R E T 2

Self-awareness can help you discover your passion.

Passion *n.* a strong liking or desire for or devotion to some activity, object, or concept

Self-awareness or **self-knowledge** may sound like an abstract concept, the stuff that poets and artists think about, but getting to know yourself is pretty much like getting to know anything else. The more you learn about something, the more it begins to make sense and the more fascinating it becomes, especially when the subject you're studying is yourself!

Self-knowledge *n.* knowledge or understanding of one's own capabilities, character, feelings, or motivations

People who know who they are—their own strengths and weaknesses, gifts and talents—are happier and more successful in life. They often feel more fulfilled because they have a purpose and a mission. They understand what makes them unique in their families, their studies, their careers, and their service to the world as a whole. They are less likely to become depressed or dependent and have a healthier network of friends.

discovering your passion

One of the best things about becoming self-aware is that it will lead you to discover your *passion*. People who know what they love to do find ways to stand out and make a difference. In the following profile, you'll read about the queen of self-awareness, and you may see why she **inspires** so many people worldwide.

Inspire *v.* to influence, spur on, or motivate; to draw forth or bring out

OPRAH WINFREY

A *passion for potential*

"My philosophy is that not only are you responsible for your life, but doing the best at this moment puts you in the best place for the next moment."

Oprah Gail Winfrey was born January 29, 1954, in Kosciusko, Mississippi. With her parents traveling to find work, Oprah was left in the care of her grandmother, Hattie Mae Lee. As a child, she went to church with her grandmother, and it was there that she discovered her talent for public speaking.

> Her first recital was at age three. From that day on, she was always the first child to be asked to recite. She recited verses and poems at churches in the Nashville area. Oprah recalls that the other women in the church would say, "Hattie Mae, that child is gifted." At age four the whole town knew that she was gifted. She became known as "the little speaker." (*Oprah Winfrey Biography*)

While still in high school and living with her father in Nashville, Oprah began her broadcasting career at a local radio station. She became the youngest person and the first African-American woman to anchor the news at Nashville's WTVF-TV. In 1984, Oprah moved to Chicago to host a morning talk show, *AM Chicago,* which became the number-one local talk show just one month after she began. In less than a year, the show was renamed *The Oprah Winfrey Show,* and it went on to become the highest-rated talk show in television history. "In 1988, she established Harpo Studios, a production facility in Chicago, making her the third woman in the American entertainment industry (after Mary Pickford and Lucille Ball) to own her own studio" (Oprah Winfrey Biography).

Today, most people know Oprah Winfrey from her weekday television show. She also publishes her own magazine, simply called *O*, and has recently launched a satellite radio program called *Oprah & Friends*. She has created several charitable organizations including the Oprah Winfrey Foundation and Oprah's Angel Network. She has personally donated millions of dollars to various causes, and she has inspired others to give millions more to other organizations.

Many people told Oprah she couldn't do the things she was attempting to do. Through it all, she was willing to work hard and believe in herself. She used her gifts and talents to build a media empire and has become a pop-culture icon as well as a beloved role model.

OPRAH.com About Oprah. www.oprah.com/about/press/about_press_bio.jhtml.
Oprah Winfrey Biography. www.angelfire.com/ne/lliegirls/WINFREY.html.

Profile Clues to Use

How did Oprah develop her abilities?

_____

_____

_____

What are some obstacles she faced?

_____

_____

_____

How do you see yourself as similar or dissimilar to her?

_____

_____

_____

LISA KNOPPE-REED

Art for a Cause

Another person who gives back in a unique way is Lisa Knoppe-Reed, founder and CEO of Art for a Cause (*www.artforacause.com*), which trains mentally disabled children and adults to paint garden tools, creating a product line called CuteTools!™. The company also partners with schools to teach children a work ethic and basic business skills while enabling them to sell the products they've made to raise money for their organization or charity.

Lisa explains:

"I always had this gut feeling that I would make a difference, and I agonized over how to do this. I'm a self-taught artist. As a young adult, I attended craft shows where I'd display my hand-painted furniture. One day an elderly woman walked into my booth looking around like Inspector Clouseau. I could see she was trying to figure out how I created my works of art. This turned out to be a pivotal point in my journey. I asked her, 'Would you like to know how to paint a chair?' I could tell she was stunned. She couldn't believe I would share my secrets! I got so much enjoyment from that encounter that it propelled me to branch out into teaching.

"Next, I went to a community college in my area and asked if they'd like for me to offer a class on painting. They were thrilled by the idea, and the class was enormously popular. The school had a waiting list of people who wanted to register. One of the students asked if I had projects for her special needs population, and this got my wheels turning. I went to Home Depot and bought paint and as many tools as I could find. I taught them how to sand and paint the tools, things like hammers, garden tools, anything with a wooden handle. They worked so hard and took such pride in their work. When I presented them with a check their faces beamed. This was far more rewarding to me than selling!

"Today we ship our product to more than 2,500 places (Hallmark stores, specialty gift shops, upscale grocery stores, catalogs, etc.). The tools are crafted by special needs children, teens, and adults. Often I feel waves of emotion about the weight of responsibility I have to keep things growing. I feel very small compared to the enormity of the task.

"Another aspect that has been tremendously rewarding is having teens mentor the special needs adults. The teens are learning valuable life lessons from my employees. They're learning what really matters in life: That it's not always what you get, but what you give, that counts.

"One thing I'd say to anyone who has an idea: Watch out for negative people, people who tell you it won't work or it can't be done. You shouldn't let them discourage you. Another thing is I'm a survivor. My dad died when I was ten years old, and I can still remember being worried about everyone else, my mom, my siblings, even my aunts and uncles. I didn't worry about me because I had my dog, my bicycle, and my inner strength. I knew I was going to be okay.

"One of my childhood dreams was to join the circus. Much of what I do today is like that. We ship our product to trade shows and international gift fairs; we set up our show and then pack up and move on to the next event. I can actually say my childhood dream came true: I really did join the circus!"

Source: Personal communication.

Profile Clues to Use

How did Lisa develop her abilities?

_____

_____

_____

What are some obstacles she faced?

_____

_____

_____

_____

How do you see yourself as similar or dissimilar to her?

_____

_____

_____

Clowning around

One person who came even closer to joining the circus is Susan Hooper of Chicago. She started going to the circus when she was a child and fell in love with it. She describes herself as a very active child and involved in everything from swimming to dance to basketball. She was constantly busy and had to balance her education, rehearsals, practice, and various events. Having so many activities forced her to learn to manage her time.

In high school, Susan became involved in theater and worked as a stage tech. Like most high school students, she was often asked questions about her career plans and college. She started to consider seriously what she wanted to do with her life. She made a list of life goals, one of which was to learn to walk on stilts. This might seem silly compared to the goals of people who want to become doctors or lawyers, but Susan was very serious and dedicated in her love of circus performing.

Although she didn't completely run off to join the circus, Susan continued to pursue circus training while attending college to earn a social services degree. Her education was focused on an area that would allow her to help people. Her circus training with Gamma Phi Circus helped her to achieve her goal of being a performer and learning to walk on stilts. Susan also learned clowning, ballooning, fire breathing, and hair hang (hanging by her hair). During school vacations she was involved with Harper College's juggling club. She learned to juggle and added another skill to her growing list of circus abilities.

She graduated from college with a degree in social work, and continued to work as a professional clown. She works with Triton Trouper Circus and continues to practice the skills she learned while in college. She also works with Great America Theme Parks, performing as a clown in parades, festivals, parties, teaching, and other events.

Susan's story underscores the importance of following a path that's right for you. She has met many wonderful people and has used her outgoing, energetic personality to entertain. Susan's career choice may seem a little unusual to a lot of people, but it's just right for her.

discovering who you are takes time

Throughout your life's journey, you will discover your talents and gifts, as well as your unique personality traits, strengths, weaknesses, passions, areas in which you struggle, and areas in which you excel. All of these discoveries take time. Be patient with the process. Learning who you are is an exploration in which you will find things you like about yourself and things you don't like about yourself.

Discovering the good and bad of who you are can be difficult. No one wants to realize that they have faults or weaknesses, and it may be hard to become aware of those weaknesses. Just remember that everyone has weaknesses and faults. What is important is that you recognize and accept the good and the bad and then learn to improve or compensate for your shortcomings.

Knowing how you naturally feel about things and what you are interested in (or not interested in) is part of understanding who you are. Everyone is different. Some people love to go out every night and meet new people. Other people like to stay in with a good book. One is not better than the other; people are just different.

When you understand what you want to do or what you are good at doing, you will be more successful in school, at work, and in relationships. For example, in school you can choose to focus on the subjects that you enjoy because, most likely, those subjects are the ones you are naturally gifted at. After graduating, you can choose a career based on your gifts. If you know that you are an introvert and you don't like meeting new people, then you can figure out that you probably would not be happy working as a shoe salesperson. Knowing that you are an introvert could also help you choose relationships. Maybe you want friends who like to sit and read books like you do, or maybe you prefer friends who are extroverts who will encourage you to go out more. Understanding who you are is the best way to discover your gifts and talents.

What do you know about yourself? The following will help you find out.

Describe yourself. Circle the traits below that best describe you.

Confident	Hard worker	Introvert
Trusting	Motivated	Extrovert
Passionate	Laid-back	Spontaneous
Focused	Carefree	Fun
Sensitive	Serious	Responsible
Leader	Organized	Dependent
High energy	Talkative	Independent
Listener	Creative	Logical

Can you think about which jobs or careers would be well-suited to the different personal traits listed here? For instance, a counselor would need to be a good listener.

Your social style

Understanding your social style is another important piece of self-awareness. Knowing how you react in social situations, and being able to identify the social settings you enjoy the most, helps you choose the situations where you put yourself. Some people love to socialize, so they like go to parties where they can meet new people and talk all night. Other people would prefer to talk with a close friend over a cup of coffee and have deep intellectual conversations. These different social styles are a big part of who you are because they can dictate who your friends are and the type of life you lead. Your social style is also related to your gifts and talents, because usually the things you enjoy doing socially are connected to your talents.

Describe your social style. Circle the styles that best describe you.

Homebody	Philanthropist	Sports enthusiast
Family oriented	Jet-setter	Part-time socializer
Late night raver	Party thrower	Party avoider
Networker	Nature lover	Introvert
Enjoys small parties	Enjoys big parties	Extrovert
Flirter	Movie buff	Shy

Gifts that come naturally

Knowing your social style is one way to get to know your gifts and talents. Some gifts develop with age, but some are things you have been good at your entire life and just come naturally. Being aware of your gifts and talents is the best way to find out what you are good at or what you might be happy doing one day. If you can find a career that is focused around one of your gifts, you will most likely enjoy your work and be good at it. What are some areas in which you have gifts and talents right now?

Unwrap your gifts. Circle the areas in which you have gifts.

Music	Painting	Mathematics
Writing	Drawing	Science
History	Athletics	Entrepreneurship
Creativity	Innovation	Building
Engineering	Mechanics	Animals
Leadership	Politics	Sculpting
Photography	Journalism	Reading
Communications	Negotiating	Comedy
Organizing	Managing	Instigating
Singing	Technology	Inventing

ikes and dislikes

Every one of us is born with gifts and talents that come naturally. In fact, they often come so naturally that you don't notice that not everyone can do them as easily or as well as you. Things that come easily to you can be a source of joy in your life, as well as a practical help to others.

At the opposite end of the spectrum are those things you dislike doing. While you might not realize it yet, knowing what you *don't* like to do can be just as important as knowing what you do like. When an activity or experience is a turn-off, that's another important clue to who you are. The following list of self-discovery questions can help you think more deeply about your likes and dislikes.

SELF-DISCOVERY QUESTIONS

When you were little, how did you like to spend your time?

_____

_____

_____

What was your favorite play activity?

_____

What did you like to do in pre-school?

_____

_____

What did you deliberately avoid doing?

_____

_____

Did you enjoy playing quietly by yourself, or did you prefer to be with others most of the time?

_____

What do you like to spend your free time doing now?

_____

_____

_____

What are your favorite subjects in school?

_____

_____

_____

What subjects do you struggle with?

_____

_____

_____

What are the characteristics of your favorite teachers?

_____

_____

_____

What are the characteristics of teachers you struggle with the most?

_____

_____

_____

What one thing interests you more than any other?

_____

If you had a way to spend a weekend or a day doing something you enjoy, would you work with people, information, or things?

_____

When you ask your best friend to describe what is special about you compared with everyone else, what does he or she say? If you have never asked, ask now!

_____

_____

_____

What one person from TV, books, history, or popular culture do you admire the most?

_____

What appeals to you about this person?

_____

_____

If you had to name one gift and/or talent that you have at this moment, what is it?

_____

_____

Following are two more questions that can help you see yourself objectively. In each case, evaluate statements A and B and select the one that sounds more like you.

Would you describe yourself as more task-oriented or people-oriented? Task-oriented people are usually focused on seeing specific results. They like closure and being able to see what they've accomplished. They tend to be focused, intense, serious, and tough-minded when it comes to money.

A task-oriented person can have just as great a love for helping others as anyone but would prefer to perform that help by doing something that does not involve direct contact with other people. For instance, a task-oriented person might be great at organizing a relief effort for hurricane victims, but this person wouldn't want to be responsible for actually distributing the items to the survivors.

○ A. I am motivated more toward completing tasks.

Those who are more **people-oriented** are usually warm, accepting, agreeable, relaxed, sensitive to the feelings of others, trusting, open, soft-hearted, less time-sensitive, and less pressed for closure. They enjoy direct contact with all kinds of people in almost any situation.

○ B. I am motivated more toward the needs of people.

Are you more outgoing or reserved? Outgoing people (extroverts) are usually talkative and generally focus on getting others to do something by persuading, directing, motivating, encouraging, leading, delegating, and discussing. Extroverts are energized by being around other people.

    ○ A. I tend to be outgoing (extroverted) in my thinking and actions.

Reserved people (introverts) generally focus on thoughts and activities related to their own performance and personal world rather than others. They prefer to contemplate, study, analyze, listen, follow instructions, and focus on the task at hand. They are energized by being alone rather than being with other people.

    ○ B. I tend to be reserved (introspective) in my thinking and actions.

The bigger picture

Have you ever looked at the moon through a telescope? Through a telescope, you are able to see details that you might otherwise miss. However, if you view the moon only in its magnified form, you might overlook how it fits into the greater context of the night sky. To fully appreciate the moon, it helps to view it up close as well as far away.

Your life has similar dimensions, and it needs to be looked at from as many angles as possible. By pulling back and looking at the bigger picture of who you are, you get a clearer view of your specific gifts and talents and how they might be used in the world at large.

One reason it is so important to look at the bigger picture is because school, where you spend the majority of your time, develops mainly just your academic abilities. While learning is obviously very important in life, your emotional and social growth are just as important.

e motional and social maturity

Have you ever known someone who was book smart but had little common sense, ability to control their emotions, or social skills? They may get straight A's and take advanced placement classes, but they may also have difficulty getting along with people or managing their personal life.

Emotional smarts involve how well you understand your feelings and the feelings of other people. It's the ability to read between the lines of what someone's saying and what they actually mean. Such as when you ask your friend, "Is something bothering you?" and she responds, "No, nothing," even though you can see she's about to cry.

Perhaps you've been in a situation yourself when you were unsure of why you behaved the way you did. Sometimes we do not understand ourselves. Have you been in situations where you felt resentful, selfish, dishonest, or afraid? The acronym RSDA comes from the first letter of each of these emotions; it is used by Al-Anon to help people identify their emotions in difficult situations. Fear is the root of all these emotions, so if you are in a situation in which you are overcome by any strong emotions, you may just be really afraid.

Can you remember a situation in which you felt negative emotions? Describe the situation and explain why or how you felt (feel free to write in emotions other than, or in addition to, the ones listed):

Situation: _____

_____

_____

_____

Resentful: _____

_____

Selfish: _____

_____

Dishonest: _____

_____

Afraid: _____

_____

Being able to understand what you are actually feeling, especially in difficult or stressful situations, can help you handle things better and understand yourself better.

LifeBound (www.lifebound.com) has published a book titled ***People Smarts for Teenagers: Becoming Emotionally Intelligent*** (2006), which explains the importance of emotional and social intelligence. Social intelligence involves connecting to others, even those people who may seem different from you, so that you can enjoy your life and be more successful. Whether it's accomplishing a project at school, thinking through a math problem, or making the most of an opportunity, your emotional and social maturity play a crucial part in discovering and developing your gifts and talents; making these discoveries requires more than mental skill alone.

Therefore, no matter what you love and what you decide to develop within yourself as you grow older and wiser, you will need to develop a love for learning along with emotional and social intelligence. We'll look at what this means in the chapters that follow.

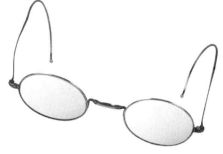

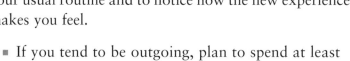

Outside your comfort zone

The purpose of this activity is to help you get outside your usual routine and to notice how the new experience makes you feel.

- If you tend to be outgoing, plan to spend at least one hour alone this week.

What did you do during this hour? How does being alone make you feel?

_____

_____

_____

_____

- If you tend to be introverted, plan to attend a new social activity this week, or initiate a conversation with someone you've never met.

What did the activity entail? How did being with other people make you feel?

_____

_____

_____

diving deep into your gifts and talents

"Practice makes perfect."

—AUTHOR UNKNOWN

Live in the moment, but prepare for your future.

Expert *n.* one who has special skill or knowledge; a specialist

You may have heard the expression, "Use it or lose it." This phrase applies to almost every area of life. When we don't exercise our muscles, they become weak and flabby. When we don't practice a musical instrument very often, we can't play it as well as if we had practiced regularly. This is also true of our gifts and talents. If they aren't used, they'll never grow.

People who fail to develop their gifts never know what they are capable of. They stand on the sidelines without risking what it takes to really know where they can go with their **innate** strengths. Home-schooled 16-year-old Nina of Cicero, Illinois, describes her "go ahead and try it attitude" to ska music.

Innate *adj.* existing in, belonging to, or determined by factors present in an individual from birth

Ska *n.* popular music of Jamaican origin that combines elements of traditional Caribbean rhythms and jazz

I was first exposed to ska when I started hanging out with a group of homeschoolers who were a few years older than me and very enthusiastic ska fans. We went to concerts all the time, and a couple of my friends were forming a band. After numerous genre changes, they finally settled on playing ska music. A few members came and went, and only the original three founding members remained constant.

After a few months, I was offered a spot in the band if I could learn how to play the trombone. I was thrilled, but of course knew nothing about the trombone, except that it was one of those musical instruments that requires years of study and practice. After being switched around by my new band mates from instrument to instrument a few times and finally ending up back at the trombone, I borrowed one from a friend's father and started taking lessons. It definitely was not very easy, but it helped that I had previously played the piano for three years, and through practice I became comfortable enough to be able to begin playing shows with them.

When I first started, I was only joining the rest of the band on stage for two songs, as those were the only two for which trombone parts had yet been written. As I learned more things to play, I worked my way up and now have performed in over a dozen concerts.

Ska is a style of music that centers mainly around being light-hearted and having a good time, so I think that as far as being in a band goes, no other style could be more fun. From road trips for out-of-town concerts to a group effort to winterize our old recording studio, my experience playing the trombone in the ska band has been great.

applemania

Elliot Carter knows a thing or two about Apples, and we're not talking about fruit. At age 14, he's quite adept at using Macs and iPods and says that Apple products "foster his creativity." Elliot says he prefers the Macintosh platform and loves the Apple culture.

Elliot has found others who share his passion: "Apple has lots of fanatical users who are cool people like movie producers, artists and musicians," he says. It's a culture that helps him "see how I can pursue artistic abilities using technology in a future career."

Elliot's passion for computers is perhaps best revealed by what happened to him in the spring of 2006. Hospitalized for two weeks following an accident, Elliot's first request upon regaining consciousness was for his laptop. "I could contact my friends and family. It was a way to have some control of my situation," he says.

Elliot has two pieces of advice for other teens who want to discover their gifts and talents: Follow what you love to do and connect with other people who share your interests. "It's great to feel a connection to something you love," he says.

So don't be afraid to become the resident expert on coins, cars, rocks, reptiles, rodents, ancient Egypt, hip-hop, sign language, sewing, or whatever else excites you.

the value of commitment

One reason it is important to develop a level of expertise *before* you see what you can do with many different areas is because it allows you to commit to a process. It is human nature to sometimes want to skip steps and head right for the prize. However, few people who are really good at what they do take shortcuts. Instead, they take their passion seriously by learning all they can and practicing their skills. In short, they work hard and take their talent as far as it can go. Sometimes people sell themselves short and don't stick with something long enough to see how far their abilities can take them. They give up too soon. Your aim is to develop **competence.**

Competence *n.* having the requisite qualities or abilities to develop or function in a particular way

Skipping steps in a process is like cheating during a test or on homework. It may get you the desired result, but it won't stretch you to see what you are really capable of doing on your own. In the long run you won't feel good about yourself because it will affect your ability to respect yourself. Following are three examples of people who developed competence in their individual areas of talent.

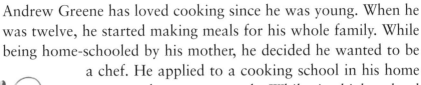

Andrew Greene has loved cooking since he was young. When he was twelve, he started making meals for his whole family. While being home-schooled by his mother, he decided he wanted to be a chef. He applied to a cooking school in his home town and was accepted. While in high school Andrew entered a national competition for his pan roasted chicken breast with spinach and blue cheese stuffing on vanilla sweet potato. This recipe, which he dreamed up all on his own, won several national awards. He is now applying to culinary schools for college.

Asante George's mother fostered her daughter's creativity by buying embroidery and plastic needlepoint kits, paints, yarn, and other craft items for her. When she was 9, Asante became interested in crocheting. By the time she was 12, she was making crocheted and beaded gifts for her family and friends. At 17, she began selling her crafts at local health food stores and import shops. She continued doing this until she came up with a plan to start her own business in which she sold her wares to high-fashion boutiques. Today, she supports herself with her craft business, selling fashion accessories such as earrings, hats, and decorative belts.

Alexandra Jewell has always loved to express herself. When she was 6 years old, she told her parents that she wanted to dance. Shortly thereafter, her father enrolled her in classes. A few years later, Alex began performing in musicals and plays. In high school and college she continued performing, taking on roles in plays, musicals, and student films. She also took roles as extras in larger films. Currently, Alex tours with a dance troupe and inspires others who are interested in the fine arts.

earning styles (and their impact on gifts and talents)

As these stories show, developing expertise in anything means having a willingness to learn and to work at it. No two people learn exactly the same way. Each person has his or her own *learning style,* which describes how each of us most effectively assimilates information and experiences. For instance, not everyone can learn from solely listening to a lecture. Some people need to involve their other senses in the learning process. Once you know how you best learn, you can figure out methods that will make learning easier.

Three basic learning styles exist. Below are brief descriptions of each. Read through them and see which description fits you best. Don't worry if you fit into more than one learning style. People can absorb new information and experiences using all of their senses. However, each person has a learning preference, and knowing this preference can help make learning *easier.*

- **Kinesthetic learner:** Kinesthetic learners learn best when their body is involved in learning. Professional athletes are the ultimate example (see the profile story later in this chapter on Venus and Serena Williams). When sitting in class, kinesthetic learners may shuffle their feet, reposition themselves often in their seat, and/or tap their fingers on their desk. Many kinesthetic learners gesture with their hands while talking. They enjoy activities that involve movement, such as sports or dancing. It can be difficult for them to concentrate when there is no external stimulus because kinesthetic learners tend to be hands-on doers, people for whom direct contact and interaction is key to learning. Many kinesthetic learners work with tools. They may like to sculpt, create art, or repair things.

Career examples: Sign language instructor, surgeon, dancer, car mechanic, gym coach, physical therapist, professional clown, stand-up comedian, art teacher, personal fitness trainer, animal trainer, forester, zoo keeper.

- **Visual learner:** Visual learners most effectively learn through seeing. They often can picture things in their mind and recall those pictures later when it comes time to take a quiz or test. Charts, diagrams, and illustrations are helpful to this type of learner. Many visual learners take detailed notes in class and may draw pictures in the margins of their paper. They tend to enjoy the visual arts and remember best through imagery. Watching someone else do something before actually doing it themselves is central to their learning process. Visual learners tend to get bored easily by lectures or anything without visual stimulation.

Career examples: Film director, television producer, web designer, media campaign planner, theater producer, museum curator, chemist, doctor.

- **Auditory learner:** Auditory learners learn best by listening or hearing. They often use rhythm to memorize things and may develop musical talents. They may prefer listening to lectures rather than watching a video. Being told how to do something is better than being shown how to do something. Auditory learners may have the ability to develop strong language skills and can carry on interesting and articulate conversations. From listening, auditory learners can accurately recall details from conversations or lectures. They may find it helpful to tape lectures and replay the tape later to compare with their notes.

Career examples: Professional musician, music teacher, radio show producer, news reporter, actor or actress, instrumentalist, composer, motivational speaker, talk-show host.

Understanding how you learn is an important aspect of discovering how to cater to your strengths. One way to better understand your learning style is to consider the obvious: How does the human brain work? The brain is a complex organ that controls our methods of learning. Although each brain is constructed similarly, the way we use it varies from individual to individual.

The brain contains two cerebral hemispheres, the left and the right. The left hemisphere controls motor skills on the right side of the body, and the right hemisphere controls motor skills on the left side of the body. Although no two brains are exactly alike, quite often the left hemisphere controls language, math, and logic, while the right hemisphere controls visual recognition, imagery, spatial abilities, and music.

LEFT HEMISPHERE		RIGHT HEMISPHERE
Language		Visual recognition
Math		Imagery
Logic		Spatial abilities
		Music

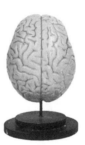

Everybody uses both brain hemispheres. Yet for many people one side is more dominant than the other. What does this mean? It is very likely that your strengths and weaknesses correspond with the dominant hemisphere. Examining the specific differences between the hemispheres can help you understand how you learn most effectively.

Those people whose left hemisphere is dominant often rely on organization and structure. Goals are completed most efficiently when tasks are worked on one at a time. People with left hemisphere dominance often do well on objective tests and like to arrange things in chronological order or in some other system. Oral expression tends to come easily for them.

When the right hemisphere is dominant, structure and organization are less of a priority. Visuals often enable clearest **comprehension** (visual learning), and multi-tasking is an effective way to accomplish tasks and goals. Those with right hemisphere dominance often do best on nonobjective, short-answer exams. Self-expression through oral communication is sometimes difficult, even though the individual understands feelings, ideas, and beliefs.

Comprehension *n.* the capacity for understanding fully

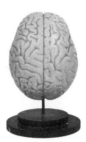

LEFT DOMINANCE	RIGHT DOMINANCE
Organization and structure	Visual learning
Single tasking	Multi-tasking
Chronological order	Nonobjective testing
Objective testing	Artistic expression

Learning styles, intelligences, and personalities combine in such a way that there are no clear cut rules regarding a person's gifts and talents. Because everyone is unique, learning strengths and personality traits also vary. It is important to note that a person with left hemisphere dominance can be a talented artist, or a person with right hemisphere dominance can be great at math. A person with right hemisphere dominance may be skilled at oral communication, and a person with left hemisphere dominance may prefer multi-tasking over single-tasking.

Sources: "Neuroscience for Kids": http://faculty.washington.edu/chudler/split.html, accessed 10/19/05; www.mtsu.edu/~studskl/hd/hemis/html, accessed 10/19/05; http://serendip.brynmawr.edu/biology/b103/f00/web2/smith2.html, accessed 10/19/05; Kinesthetic Learners Info: www2.yk.psu.edu/learncenter/acskills/kinesthetic.html, accessed 10/22/05; LifeBound's: *Study Skills* Visual Learners; www2.yk.psu.edu/learncenter/acskills/visual.html, accessed 10/22/05; Auditory Learners Info: www2.yk.psu.edu/learncenter/acskills/auditory.html, accessed 10/22/05.

SELF-DISCOVERY QUESTIONS

What techniques help you learn most effectively?

_____

_____

What study methods would you like to try to help you learn? Take a moment to brainstorm ideas.

_____

_____

How can you apply these learning techniques to your school work? For example, when studying math, do you prefer visuals, such as charts or graphs, or do you perform better with written or verbal instructions?

_____

_____

_____

How can you exercise your talents using learning techniques? For example, if you are an athlete, is it easier to learn a play by ordering the moves in sequence, or by seeing the play visually? If you are an artist, do you like to create artwork containing organizational elements, or do you prefer to create art with less order?

_____

_____

_____

As we consider dual sides of the human brain, here is a profile story about two sisters who developed expertise on the tennis court.

VENUS AND SERENA WILLIAMS

Dynamic duo

"Growing up we had a lot of insecurities."

—SERENA WILLIAMS

Venus and Serena's father, Richard Williams, loved tennis and, despite not having any practical coaching or competitive experience, decided to teach his daughters how to play. Richard managed and coached the girls because, from an early age, they clearly were interested in the game. They practiced on public courts in their hometown of Compton, California, a suburb of Los Angeles. Could a man who had never competed in tennis help to foster two top-ranked players?

Against the odds, the girls' passion for the game, their willingness to work hard, and their family's support put them on the fast track to success. In 1991, Richard made one of his more controversial decisions concerning his daughters' careers; he took them off the junior circuit and started them on the senior. "Richard Williams has said that he hoped to avoid subjecting his daughters to competitive pressures, including an undertone of racial hostility."

Richard again surprised the tennis circuit when he allowed the girls to turn pro. They were so young that Venus made her professional debut in Canada because she was too young to play professional tennis in the United States. She lost in less than an hour to a low-ranked player. Instead of being discouraged and giving up, Richard gave his daughters constant encouragement.

The sisters' list of professional accomplishments is extraordinary. When Venus won the Wimbledon championship in 2000, she joined Serena, who had won the 1999 U.S. Open, as a Grand Slam winner. It was the first time in tennis history that two sisters each had won a Grand Slam singles title. In the 2000 Olympics, they became the first sisters to win the Olympic doubles event. From July through October 15, 2000, Serena and Venus won eight of the nine tournaments they entered.

The sisters have been featured on *Oprah* with their book, *Venus and Serena: Serving from the Hip: 10 Rules for Living, Loving, and Winning,* which is a guide to empower teenage girls. During the interview in 2005, they talked about overcoming challenges and making dreams come true in spite of overwhelming odds. "That's why we wanted to get together and write a book for teenagers who deal with the same issues. [We wanted] to let them know that celebrities and stars, not only just us, but everyone, has these issues as well," Serena told Oprah.

Sources: www.oprah.com/tows/slide/200503/20050330/slide_20050330_101.jhtml.

411 on Serena bio, Serena Williams Official Website, 7 June 2006, www.serenawilliams.com/content/default.sps?iType=5099.

"Serena Williams," Contemporary Black Biography, Vol. 41, Thomson Gale, 7 June 2006, www.galegroup.com/free_resources/bhm/bio/williams_s.htm.

Profile Clues to Use

How did Venus and Serena Williams develop their abilities?

_____

_____

_____

_____

What are some obstacles they faced?

_____

_____

_____

_____

How do you see yourself as similar or dissimilar to them?

_____

_____

_____

_____

book smarts

We could say that the Williams sisters embody kinesthetic intelligence, with right hemisphere dominance. Following is an example of someone with linguistic intelligence.

At nine months old, Jennifer was already quite verbal, indicating left hemisphere dominance. She could talk and even recite simple nursery rhymes that her mother taught her. Now in her twenties, Jennifer works as a children's librarian at Fox River Grove Memorial Library in Illinois. She loves her career and has many responsibilities. Jennifer's journey to becoming a children's librarian has spanned all the years of her life, but she would tell you that her hard work and efforts have paid off.

While in high school Jennifer got a job at her hometown library. Because she was so passionate about her job, she was invited back to work at the library every summer. After high school graduation, Jennifer enrolled at Columbia College in Illinois. Like most people, Jennifer did not enter college knowing exactly what she wanted to become. Because she loves to write, Jennifer decided to earn her bachelor's degree in fiction writing.

As graduation drew near, Jennifer considered a career in teaching because she loves

working with children, but she ultimately decided that a career in teaching was not for her. Jennifer chose to follow her instinct and become a children's librarian. Her past summer work experience demonstrated that a career as a librarian would allow her to combine her love for reading and writing and also enable her to work closely with children.

In order to become a librarian, Jennifer needed to earn a master's degree in library and information science. Someone who earns this degree can become a librarian at a public, medical, school, university, or corporate library. Jennifer still hoped to pursue a career as a children's librarian at a public library. Instead of taking a year off from school in order to work and earn money, she decided to go straight to graduate school.

Jennifer found this quick transition between college and graduate school to be somewhat overwhelming. Government grants no longer funded her education, and she struggled to pay her way through school. At times, she felt a great deal of self-doubt. "I kept pushing myself through, knowing that the end of each semester meant I was getting closer and closer to graduation." Jennifer's hard work paid off. Soon after earning her master's degree, Jennifer was hired to be a children's librarian.

Jennifer loves her career because she is able to combine many of her interests in reading, writing, and art. She works with kids of all ages. Among a long list of responsibilities, Jennifer orders books, runs programs, creates newsletters, and manages the library's website. She formed a monthly creative writing group for both children and adults, and she holds "poetry slams" at coffee shops. Jennifer also enjoys her job because the kids she works with choose to come to the library; they share Jennifer's passion for reading. Jennifer does not consider her career as a librarian to be work. "It doesn't feel like work at all to me. I'm constantly doing new things and seeing new people. I get to do everything that I love to do," she says.

The following profile story is about someone else who loves books. The only difference is that she doesn't just read them; she writes them!

AMY TAN

Closing the generation gap

"I think books were my salvation—they saved me from being miserable."

A my Tan was born in California in 1952, the daughter of Chinese immigrants. Her early years were characterized by conflict with her mother and national turmoil. Her parents had immigrated to escape the Chinese Civil War.

As in some mother–daughter relationships, Amy and her mother, Daisy, didn't understand each other. Their problems were exacerbated by the clash of cultures between Amy who was raised in the West and her Chinese mother. Amy liked to resolve conflict by discussing issues in a direct manner. This didn't square with Daisy, who tended to respond better to an indirect communication style. While she was in college, Amy decided to study English; Daisy wanted her daughter to study medicine.

Amy's advanced studies in linguistics and an interest in helping children led to jobs as a language development consultant and later as director for a nonprofit training project for developmentally disabled children. Amy decided to make a dramatic shift in her career by becoming a freelance business writer because it paid better than working for a nonprofit organization. Over time, she secured well-paying jobs with large companies.

A short time later, Amy's mother became seriously ill. Amy promised herself that if her mother recovered, she would take Daisy to China once again. Her mother did recover and the trip was a revelation for Amy. "It gave her a new perspective on her often-difficult relationship with her mother" (Academy of Achievement website). She completed a book of stories about Chinese women titled *The Joy Luck Club*, which spent eight months on the *New York Times* best-seller list. Since then, she's written several other books and two children's stories focusing on the lives of Chinese immigrants.

Amy was willing to defy tradition to pursue her gifts. She made a drastic and even risky change from business writing to writing fiction. Her success as a fiction writer came about in large part due to her willingness to see things from another person's perspective, her mother's.

Amy had to be willing to set aside anger and hurt and look at the world with fresh eyes. Perhaps one of the biggest challenges anyone faces is to see someone they know and love in a new way. This ability to open her heart led Amy to a greater understanding of Daisy's life and culture—an understanding she has eloquently shared with the world in her books.

Academy of Achievement website. Amy Tan. www.achievement.org/autodoc/page/tan0bio-1.
Amy Tan's website, www.amytan.net/home.aspx; BIO.

Profile Clues to Use

How did Amy Tan develop her abilities?

_____

_____

_____

_____

What are some obstacles she faced?

_____

_____

_____

_____

How do you see yourself as similar or dissimilar to her?

_____

_____

_____

_____

_____

SELF-DISCOVERY ACTIVITY

Create a plan

What talent would you like to develop? Write out a plan for ways you can develop this gift by increasing your practice time and learning more about it. If you need some help, interview an expert in the field. This could be a family friend, someone in your community or at your school, and so on. Below are some ideas to help you get started and a questionnaire for the person you'd like to interview. Feel free to come up with your own questions, too!

The ability or talent I would like to develop is

_____

_____

_____

One thing I can do this week to develop my gift is

_____

_____

_____

CHAPTER THREE

One resource I can check out to learn more about my gift or talent is

_____

_____

One person I can talk to about my desire to develop my ability is

_____

_____

Interview questionnaire

How did you discover your gifts and abilities?

_____

_____

_____

Who helped you improve in your area of giftedness?

_____

_____

_____

What was the biggest fear or obstacle you had to overcome to develop your talent?

_____

_____

_____

CHAPTER

4

expanding

MATCHING YOUR GIFTS AND TALENTS TO CAREERS

"The universe is a big place. But it's okay—
you'll grow into it."

—CARL MUNSON, NUTRITIONIST AND AUTHOR

S E C R E T 4

Use all the tools at your fingertips to achieve your dreams.

Resource *n.* A source of supply or support;
a source of information or expertise

As a child, Merl Reagle loved crossword puzzles and word scrambles. In his teenage years, he would scramble his friends' names. He called one of his good friends, Tim Fuller, "Full Timer" (although, Merl says, "it wasn't really much of a scramble—I just stuck his first name inside his last name"). He spelled my name, Carol Carter, backward and called me Retrac Lorac.

Reagle is featured in the 2006 movie *Wordplay.* In one scene he drives past a famous donut shop and says: "Dunkin Donuts . . . put the D at the end and you get UNKIND DONUTS . . . which I've had a few of in my day."

Who would have guessed when Merl was a child that he would have a fabulous career writing crossword puzzles for the *New York Times,* the *Los Angeles Times,* the *Philadelphia Inquirer,* the *San Francisco Chronicle,* and many other publications? And that he would be the author of 12 best-selling crossword puzzle books? It just goes to show, when you pay attention to what you love, and you work hard to cultivate a competence in that area, you can turn it into meaningful work.

Once you have a sense of what you love to do, and you have begun to develop a deep and thorough expertise in that area, you will be ready for the next step: seeing the broad and numerous ways that you can use your gifts and talents. Fortunately, many resources can help you match your gifts and talents to various jobs or career fields. Tapping these resources will help you develop a high level of what guidance counselors call "career literacy." Here is a list of some of these resources:

- Internet
- School and public libraries

- Your school's career guidance center
- Parents
- Teachers and coaches
- Neighbors
- Community leaders
- Summer jobs

O nward!

Remember my story from Chapter 1? Let's take that as an example of what someone can do with my talents: love for people and talking with people. First, use your own creative juices to brainstorm three careers that I could go into with what I am good at:

_____

_____

_____

How did you do? If it was hard for you, don't worry. Learning to brainstorm is one of the skills this book is designed to teach because the capacity to generate ideas will help you in whatever career you decide to pursue. To help you feel better, it was hard for me to even know three things I could do while I was in high school. Here are the various things I would be qualified to do if I developed my expertise in these areas:

News anchorperson	Sales person
Radio talk show host	Marketing manager
Newsroom reporter	Sales manager
Field interviewer	Retail sales person
Public relations specialist	Teacher
Speech writer	Corporate trainer
Motivational speaker	Counselor
Lawyer	Social worker

Some of these careers may be unfamiliar to you. That is okay. The one thing they all have in common is that they involve working with people and talking to people. In addition, many of these areas also involve persuading and influencing others. Isn't it cool to see how much you can do with one thing you are good at? I am skilled at a few other things, too, so this list explores only one area of my gifts and talents.

It should be comforting for you to know that, with your gifts and talents, there are hundreds or possibly even thousands of jobs for which you would be suitable. Many high school students become unnecessarily stressed out because they either can't think of anything they are talented at doing or they don't realize how many options are actually out there with the gifts and talents they have. A little investigative work can reveal all these things.

The nice part is that you don't need to make any big decisions right now. You just need to be aware that you can do many great things to shape your abilities as time goes on. You need to commit to playing these innate strengths of yours to their fullest. Here's a prime example of what we're talking about.

CRAIG NEWMARK

Internet mogul

"The secret is, just treat other people like you want to be treated."

Although you may not know anything about Craig Newmark, you've probably heard about his wildly popular website craigslist.com, where you can find anything from a ferret to a Ferrari. Craigslist started in 1995 as a community service based in San Francisco. Today it's worth hundreds of millions of dollars and serves more than 10 million people a month. Here's how it happened, according to Craig:

I decided that I would start sending people notices about cool events, usually ones that involved arts and technology. And from there, via word of mouth, the news of the list spread. People wanted to be added. People wanted more stuff like jobs or stuff to sell posted there. And then I said "how 'bout apartments?" and it just grew like that. People wanted more, had suggestions. We did it. And that's the pattern to this day. (Johnsville.blogspot.com)

In June 2006, Craig was interviewed on NBC's *Today Show.* The show's correspondent said, "What we found does not exactly fit the image of an Internet mogul." Craig dresses simply, takes the trolley to work every day, and lives in a "fancy shack" in San Francisco. He compares himself to the cartoon strip character Dilbert, a nerdy office worker. Nevertheless, despite his simple habits, craigslist is one of the largest online companies in the world.

Craig grew up in Morristown, New Jersey, where he was co-captain of the debate team in high school. He and some friends also started a club for playing the Asian game Go. He holds a bachelor's and a master's degree in computer science.

Several years ago, Craig, who himself wears glasses, set up a foundation that gives money to poor Israeli and Palestinian children for eye exams and eyeglasses. His personal and professional motto is "give people a break." Need a car, a job, a date? You can find almost anything or anyone, including its founder, at craigslist.com.

Sources: http://johnsville.blogspot.com/2005/08/bio-of-craig-newmark-founder-of.html. www.msnbc.msn.com/id/13439174.

Profile Clues to Use

How did Craig Newmark develop his abilities?

_____

_____

_____

What skills did he need to become successful?

_____

_____

_____

_____

What are some obstacles he had to overcome?

_____

_____

_____

_____

How do you see yourself as similar or dissimilar to him?

_____

_____

_____

_____

Other suggestions for building "career literacy"

Career *n.* a profession for which one trains and that is undertaken as a permanent calling

Job *n.* a position in which one is employed

Various stages of school

Middle school. Here are some suggestions for what to do, or what to look for, when you are in middle school.

- Ask adults how they got their job, what they do, what they like and dislike about it, and what kind of training and education they needed.

- Explore services and products available in your own community. For example, how many different jobs produced the food for your dinner?

- Visit work sites and websites.

- Think about what you see in the media. What is realistic? What is the real situation (if the media portrayal is not realistic)?

- When visiting a doctor's office or clinic, observe what types of employees work there. What type of education do they need to do their job?

- Interview people you admire and ask them about their career paths.

- Seek job-shadowing opportunities.

High school. Here are some suggestions for how to learn about various careers while you are in high school.

- Consider getting a comprehensive career assessment and having it interpreted by a credentialed career professional.

- Investigate how creativity is used in the workplace in fields other than art. What different types of designers can you identify?

- When interviewing colleges, ask to speak with alumni in your intended major to find out how their education fit in different careers.

- Become familiar with online resources that provide basic information about careers, projected availability, requirements, and salary.

- Recognize that teamwork is required in today's workplace. Performing community service, helping others, and working on a project offer opportunities to stretch those inter-personal talents.

- Brainstorm with a counselor or a career coach.
- Seek a summer job.

Summer jobs

Being employed is another sure way to discover and develop your gifts and talents. Work also teaches you responsibility, marketable skills, and money management. What kind of jobs can a teen expect to get? We've divided the world of teen jobs into two categories: minimum-wage jobs and all others. Let's start with a look at the minimum-wage jobs. Here is a list of common jobs for teens:

fast food cook or cashier	lawn care provider
retail stocker or sales clerk	snow shoveler
grocery store bagger	gas station attendant
companion for the elderly	baby sitter
restaurant—bus person or hostess	pet sitter
movie theater cleaner	car washer
movie theater concession salesperson	house cleaner
	lifeguard

Here is a list of other jobs that may provide more pay based on your experience, maturity level, and willingness to go beyond what's expected:

sports instructor	personal assistant (requires driving)
web designer	
childcare/nanny	telemarketer
office assistant/filer	receptionist
movie-ticket clerk	hostess
house/commercial painter	cook
worker at a day spa or retreat center	dishwasher

Many students begin with a minimum-wage job, prove themselves, and then progress to more lucrative work where pay may be as high as $10 to $15 an hour. To command this level of wage, a teen usually must demonstrate extraordinary drive and talent.

Of course, work experience isn't the only way to match your talent to future careers. Summer camps and enrichment programs can also help you connect an interest with a skill that can be used in the real world. Matt, a freshman in high school, describes such an experience:

> One of my most inspiring experiences was Earth Camp at Mount Lemmon in Tucson, Arizona. I enjoyed sharing a tent with my friends, and being out in the wilderness. We had fencing duels with sticks, card games, and explored the outdoors.
>
> This experience inspired me to be a photographer of the wilderness. There are so many cool plants, animals, and bugs that I want to photograph and be able to remember. Whether at the Desert Museum, at Kitt Peak, at Mount Lemmon, or in my back yard, I want to take pictures of the wildlife.

The following profile story shows how support from other people can also help develop your abilities to their fullest extent.

KALPANA CHAWLA

A life fully lived (1961–2003)

"It's easy for me to be motivated and inspired by seeing somebody who just goes all out to do something."

Kalpana Chawla, a NASA astronaut, became the first Indian-born woman to travel into space. She worked hard to achieve her life-long dream of becoming an aerospace engineer and astronaut; then, on February 1, 2003, while she was aboard Space Shuttle *Columbia* STS-107, the shuttle exploded and every astronaut died. *Columbia* was within sixteen minutes of its landing back on earth. This tragic event cost Kalpana her life, and that of all her colleagues. Despite her short life, Kalpana's accomplishments illustrate a life fully lived.

Kalpana always had a love for airplanes. While growing up in Karnal, India, she took an interest in the flying clubs that were dispersed throughout the area and found their planes intriguing. Upon request, their father took both Kalpana and her brother to a local flying club and arranged for a ride in the sky. Despite his encouragement of her interest in planes as a hobby, he was horrified when he learned she wanted to be a pilot. She won over her parents to the idea of her becoming a pilot when she graduated in 1982 from Punjab Engineering College, receiving a bachelor of science degree in aeronautical engineering.

Her family continued to resist her dreams, however. When she wanted to go to the United States, to earn her master's degree, her father simply said, "No." After building a life for his family (following the bloody split from British rule and the creation of Pakistan in 1947), he was the undisputed leader of the family. Nevertheless, Kalpana convinced them, and in 1984 she earned a master of science degree in aerospace engineering from the University of Texas; in 1988 she received her Ph.D. from the University of Colorado. Clearly, she dedicated many years of her life to her goal of becoming an aerospace engineer.

In 1988, directly after earning her final degree, Kalpana began working for NASA. Toward the beginning of her career, she worked predominantly on research. In 1994, she was one of 19 people selected from nearly 3,000 applicants to become an astronaut; she became an astronaut candidate at the Johnson Space Center in 1995. She held many titles and positions throughout her career and traveled to space twice, once in 1997 aboard STS-87 *Columbia,* and the second time in 2003, aboard STS-107 *Columbia.*

During the official STS-107 pre-flight interview, when asked how she had managed to fulfill her life-long goals and what had inspired her, Kalpana stated: "I think inspiration and tied with it is motivation." She discussed a number of people who had inspired her through the years, including her patient high school teachers who believed in her, and explorers whom she had always admired. Among the people who had inspired her were Lewis and Clark, acrobatic pilot Patty Wagstaff, and naturalist and author Peter Matthiessen.

After reading numerous books about the people she admired, Kalpana reflected: "When I read about these people, I think the one thing that just stands out is their perseverance in how they carried out what they wished to carry out." Kalpana was clearly intelligent and talented, but she could not have accomplished her dreams if she had not been willing to work very hard, and if she had not possessed a legacy of character from her family.

Sources: *Astronaut Biography: Kalpana Chawla.* 30 June 2005. SPACE.com. June 7, 2006. www.space.com/missionlaunches/bio_chawla.html. (Please note that this site is somewhat out of date, as it was written before the *Columbia* was launched, but it does contain some useful information.)

Joseph, Josy. *The Chawlas' Odyssey.* 7 Feb 2006. The Rediff Special. June 7, 2006. www.rediff.com/news/2003/feb/01spec.htm.

Kalpana Chawla (Ph.D.) NASA Astronaut. May 2004. National Aeronautics and Space Administration. June 7, 2006. www.jsc.nasa.gov/Bios/htmlbios/chawla.html.

Profile Clues to Use

How did Kalpana Chawla develop her abilities?

What skills did she need to become successful?

_____

_____

_____

_____

What are some obstacles she had to overcome?

_____

_____

_____

_____

How do you see yourself as similar or dissimilar to her?

_____

_____

_____

_____

S tart exploring careers early

Many adults work in jobs they hate because they aren't using their gifts. You don't want that to happen to you! Exploring careers early in life helps you become the person you are meant to be.

Some students have many interests, while others may focus their energy on only one or two interests. Still others may be unable to distinguish which activities are most important to them. So, as exciting as it is to discover where you can go with your gifts and talents, just remember that you can't go too far without developing your competence and your expertise. If you do that well, you will find that you have endless opportunities as you get older. As William Shakespeare wrote, "the world's mine oyster." Or, as we might say in modern language: The world is yours for the taking.

SELF-DISCOVERY QUESTIONS

What makes you feel fulfilled? Perhaps it's when you help someone, fix something, travel somewhere, draw, or dance. Describe the activity and the feelings and thoughts it stirs within you.

_____

_____

_____

_____

_____

_____

As noted earlier in the chapter, a career requires a substantial amount of your energy and time. You must commit yourself to becoming a lifelong learner if you want to be a respected and fully functioning expert in your career field. Ideally, everyone wants a satisfying job that they enjoy, one that allows them to use their gifts and talents to the fullest.

Choose at least two skills and/or strengths that would help you feel fulfilled if used on a daily basis during your future career:

1. _____

_____

2. _____

_____

Career search

In order to find ways to use your interests in a future career, research is necessary. The Internet is a great tool for this. Many websites provide in-depth descriptions of different careers, and through research on these sites you can discover careers that you might one day want to pursue. Websites contain many areas of focus and are sometimes confusing, so be patient and take the time to discover all the information that they cover.

When considering career opportunities, it is important to keep your options open and consider as many possibilities as you can. When beginning a career search, it is helpful to start by researching types of careers, the duties and responsibilities these positions entail, and the skills that are necessary to carry them out. On websites, such helpful job descriptions are often found under a section titled "Job Profiles." When job searching, you should not limit yourself; this is an opportunity for you to explore all areas. The sky is the limit.

entrepreneurships

In the future, you may want to establish your own business, as did Craig Newmark, who was profiled in this chapter. An entrepreneur develops a business and assumes responsibility for any financial risks that he or she may be taking by investing in the idea. Ideally, an entrepreneur should create a philosophy and belief system behind the business, as well as create a vision for the company. What are the business goals? What ideas and concepts does the business value? Creativity is key to developing a successful entrepreneurship.

Go to www.startupjournal.com/, a great website for and about entrepreneurs. Review the "How-To" stories and answer the following questions:

What entrepreneurship story interested you most, and why?

_____

_____

_____

_____

If you were going to become an entrepreneur and start your own business in the near future, what type of business would you choose to establish?

_____

_____

_____

Make a list of your company goals and values.

_____

_____

_____

_____

onster.com

Go to www.monster.com and use this site to research a market, industry, or career field of interest. Click on "Career Advice," "Jobsearch Basics," and "Job Profiles." The jobs and careers are arranged alphabetically.

In the space provided below, describe anything new that you learned about a particular career and the responsibilities that it requires.

_____

_____

_____

_____

Find two markets, industries, or career fields that somehow correspond with the interests you listed earlier. In the spaces below, provide the title and a brief description of each.

1. _____
   _____
   _____

2. _____
   _____
   _____

Outlandish jobs

Some career seekers love adventuresome jobs, like storm chasers and safari guides. Check out these web links for unusual job and career opportunities.

www.backdoorjobs.com
www.princetonreview.com/cte/articles/plan/tenjobs.asp

Here's a site for environmental jobs and "green" careers:

http://jobs.aol.com/savetheplanet

Now follow the same steps as in the monster.com exercise. Find industries or career fields that correspond with your interests, and provide the title and a brief description of each in the spaces below.

1. _____
   _____
   _____

2. _____
   _____
   _____

short- and long-term goals

" A goal is a dream with a finish line."

—DUKE ELLINGTON, JAZZ MUSICIAN

S E C R E T 5

Plans, both big and small, are the key to reaching your goals.

Harness *n.* to make use of the power or potential of; to bring under control and direct the force of

You may have heard the saying, "Aim at nothing and you'll hit it every time." A life without **goals** is like a horse without a harness or a ship without a rudder. They tend to wander aimlessly. Goals are what help you keep your eyes on the prize. Only by planning where you want to go in life can you successfully reach your personal destination.

Goal *n.* the end toward which effort is directed

Central to this plan is how you will spend your time. To develop skill in any area of life, you must practice and hone your abilities; this involves a commitment of time and energy, something we talked about in Chapter 3. This is where goal setting comes into play. Goals help you manage your time wisely so that you can achieve your personal best.

Many students think of goal-setting as a long-term affair. It is true that long-term goals are important but so are short-term goals. Short-term goals are often the foundation or starting point for long-term ones. Short-term goals also help you to have a productive day by helping you manage your time. Here's how one teen, Danny, describes his approach to setting goals:

> I do set goals for myself. My most recent goal was learning a new skateboard trick. Another goal I had was getting an A on my math test. When I achieve a goal, it feels like I got something done. I have completed something I wanted, and it feels good. A goal I am setting for myself right now is to do better in science.

S tep by step

Here is a systematic approach to setting and achieving your goals.

Make a list. Write down 5 to 10 things you would like to accomplish today. When you have accomplished each goal, check it off the list.

Carry over. Don't be upset if you have things you did not get to by the end of the day. Items that are still on your list can be carried over to tomorrow.

Be realistic. Be sure to keep your daily lists fairly small. It is easy to write page-long lists. If your daily list has more than 10 goals on it, you may become overwhelmed.

Take it a step further. Setting daily goals is a good start, but to become truly successful, you will want to set goals that take you to where you want to be. Here are six steps that will help you do just that:

1. Give yourself some time to think about what you would like to accomplish in the next year. Write down your thoughts. Be sure to be specific and thorough. Don't forget to include things such as your hobbies and interests. The list you come up with will represent your big, long-range goals.

2. When you have your list of long-range goals, take some time to prioritize them. Pick the top three or four items that mean the most to you.

3. Now, write down everything you would like to accomplish in the next three to six months. Don't forget to be thorough. This new list will represent your medium-range goals. Prioritize the list again and select the top three or four goals you consider the most important.

4. Write down all of the things you would like to accomplish this week or this month. This list represents your small, or short-term goals. Prioritize the list and choose your top three or four items.

5. Consult your list frequently. You may find it a good idea to share your list with an adult or **mentor** you trust and respect. This person may hold you accountable to following through on your goals. Checking your list frequently will keep you on track.

Mentor *n.* a trusted counselor or guide

6. Don't dismiss this effective tool. With consistence, you will find that goal-setting really works in helping you achieve your dreams.

This chapter's first profile story shows how setting goals doesn't mean being boxed into a boring or predictable routine. Goals are meant to be stepping stones to finding an interest you're passionate about. The life lesson is when you find your true passion, be ready to change your course of action!

ZANA BRISKI

Shifting perspectives

"It was the children who accepted me immediately. They didn't quite understand what I was doing there, but they were fascinated by me and my camera."

Zana Briski was born in London, England, and earned a master's degree in theology and religious studies at the University of Cambridge. In 2003, she created the award-winning documentary film *Born into Brothels*, a candid look at the lives of children of prostitutes in India. During the making of the film, she taught the kids how to use a camera and raised international awareness to the problems they face. She also formed Kids with Cameras, an organization that sells the pictures children have taken.

In *Born into Brothels,* the book that accompanies the film, Zana describes how she ended up living and working among the poorest of the poor.

> In 1998 I began living with prostitutes in a squalid red light district of Calcutta. When I first went to India, I had no idea what lay ahead as I began to travel and photograph the harsh realities of women's lives. I had no intention of photographing prostitutes until a friend took me to the red light district in Calcutta. From the moment I stepped foot inside that maze of alleyways, I knew that this was the reason I had come to India.
>
> It was the children who accepted me immediately. They didn't quite understand what I was doing there, but they were fascinated by me and my camera. I let them use it and showed them how to take pictures. I thought it would be great to see this world through their eyes. It was then that I decided to teach them photography.
>
> I gave up my own photography and began to work with the kids full time. I knew that there was something important to document here so I bought a video camera and began to film the kids in the brothels, in the streets and on photo class trips. I had never even picked up a video camera before. (*Born into Brothels*)

Zana's story teaches a great life lesson: Always be ready to change your course of action when you find your true passion. Zana discovered a love for children, and she created a work any filmmaker would be proud of. Her film can be rented or bought and her book is also available at www.kids-with-cameras.org/home.

Sources: Briski, Zana. *Born into Brothels : Photographs by the Children of Calcutta.* New York: Umbrage, 2005.

"Contributors' Bios." www.pixelpress.org/bios.html

"Meet Zana Briski & Ross Kauffman" www.eye.net/eye/issue/issue_02.17.05/film/meet.html

Profile Clues to Use

How did Zana Briski develop her passion?

_____

_____

_____

_____

_____

What are some obstacles she had to overcome?

_____

_____

_____

_____

How do you see yourself as similar or dissimilar to her?

_____

_____

_____

_____

_____

What do you admire most about Zana Briski? Why?

_____

_____

_____

_____

_____

managing time

When speaking about time, the famous Chicago poet Carl Sandburg said, "Time is the coin of your life. It is the only coin you have, and only you can determine how it will be spent. Be careful lest you let other people spend it for you." Those old-fashioned hour glasses that contain grains of sand are perhaps an accurate and graphic representation of how quickly time slips away.

How you spend your time is directly related to what you will achieve in life. Many things will clamor for your attention. Here are some tips on how to use your time to achieve your goals:

- Make a daily schedule and stick to it. For example:

7 A.M.	wake up, shower
7:30 A.M.	eat breakfast
8 A.M.–3 P.M.	go to school
4 P.M.	basketball practice
5 P.M.	start homework
6 P.M.	dinner
6:30–8 P.M.	finish homework
8–8:30 P.M.	talk to friends
8:30–9 P.M.	Review tomorrow's schedule, prepare bookbag for the next day
9:30 P.M.	sleep

- Limit the amount of time you watch TV, or play video and computer games. These are real time guzzlers.
- Ask a trusted friend or adult to be honest about how you could make better use of your time.

Let's see how Lauren, a high school student with her sights set on college, used time wisely in order to achieve her goals.

ICE DREAMS

Lauren took her first ice skating lesson when she was five. Over time her passion for ice skating increased, and she decided to take skating to a higher level. She set a goal to practice every day. By the time she was in middle school, Lauren was skating seven days a week, two hours a day, before and after school. Although she despised dragging herself out of bed around five every morning, she would be wide awake and energized by the time she hit the ice.

Lauren experienced mental blocks when she could not land a jump properly. Thinking that she would never accomplish her goal, her sense of confidence weakened. "When I had self-doubts I turned myself into a bullet. I forced myself to attempt the jumps, even if they scared me. That is the only way I could learn how to land them."

As she grew more experienced in skating and her abilities strengthened, she set a new goal—to skate competitively. She performed in many competitions, and her belief in herself grew with every one.

Lauren's parents always encouraged and supported her because they understood how much she loved skating. When she was young, they drove her back and forth to her daily lessons. For each competition, Lauren's mother made her a new, colorful skating dress with an intricate design. Lauren's closet is now full of skating dresses, each one reminding her of a different skating experience.

At 17, Lauren is now an experienced and talented ice skater. As college draws near, she plans to major in physical therapy. How does ice skating relate to physical therapy? Physical health is an integral aspect of ice skating because, in order to perform at their best, ice skaters need to be in peak physical condition. Looking back on her experience thus far with skating, Lauren explains, "I'll never be able to let go of skating. I definitely want to keep it in my life, one way, or another. I may even become a skating coach some day." She concludes, "Do something you love doing, regardless of whether or not you're initially talented at it. That is what will make your talent grow."

the power of mentoring

We all need someone to get us where we need to go and help us grow along the way. This is especially true when you're learning to stretch your wings and fly. An essay by Carolyn Wilson titled "You can't reach the sky unless someone's got your back," printed in the *West Suburban Journal* (Illinois) on December 15, 2005, makes this point:

> There is no shame in seeking support to reach your highest goals and aspirations or to walk with you through the storms of life. There are many examples of real-life pairings where obvious dependence on each other had a tremendous impact on the task at hand. As sisters, Venus and Serena Williams changed the world of tennis by supporting their mutual competitive drive even when they faced each other on opposite sides of the net.
>
> [Another example is] the Chicago Bulls duo that ruled basketball in the nineties, Michael Jordan and Scottie Pippen. I watched the retirement ceremony of Pippen's #33 joining MJ's #23 in the rafters of the United Center. It was Pippen's time to shine solo in admiration and respect from former coaches, teammates and fans. Any questions about how he honestly felt playing in MJ's shadow should be put to rest by the affection displayed in their remarks. They thanked each other for giving their best every single day, whether in practice or games to become the best that they could be. Pippen wasn't trying to "be like Mike" and Jordan respected him for all that he brought to the court and watching his back. Excelling in their gifts and embracing the other's skills brought moments of greatness and six NBA championships.
>
> A sidekick or right hand position can be invaluable when ego and self-promotion are not in the equation. When you are matched for common causes remember that both parties will stand a little taller when there is sincere effort. *(Used with permission.)*

When it comes to setting goals, sometimes it is hard to know where to start. Don't worry. Many people who have already achieved what you want to achieve are there to help you succeed.

These people can become your personal mentors. Mentors are trustworthy guides, advisors, or coaches who are often a bit older, wiser, and experienced. They will want to help you because they see that you have a passion to reach your goals. They too had people who helped them, so they understand the value of mentoring. The following true story shows how a mentor helped one girl develop her passion for photography.

PICTURE PERFECT

Alyssa's love for photography began at an early age. When she was about eight years old, her mom took her to a hot air balloon festival where she took pictures of the balloons. After being entered in a contest, her pictures were selected to be on exhibit at the town's art gallery. While she was in middle school, Alyssa and her family went out to California, where she took pictures of the giant redwoods. They also visited Yosemite National Park, and Alyssa fell in love with the photographs of Ansel Adams.

Mary Robitaille, the mother of one of Alyssa's friends, is a photographer who became Alyssa's mentor. "She helped me with everything," explains Alyssa. She discovered that she enjoys the entire process of photography. She likes being in a darkroom developing pictures, and she likes experimenting with different subjects: landscapes, black and white, and portraits.

During her junior year in high school, she assisted the photographer at a cousin's wedding. After a while, the hired photographer began to follow her around. He'd say things like, "Wow! You've found a great angle." Alyssa shot 23 rolls of film that day.

As a senior in high school, Alyssa took a new art course called "portfolio development." "I look forward to compiling my best photos and seeing where all of this will take me. My dream job would be to work for L.L. Bean taking photos for their catalog or for *National Geographic* magazine."

peers as mentors

Keep in mind that mentors don't have to be full-fledged adults. Your best mentor might be someone close to your own age who has expertise in what you want to learn or do. Think about your friends and the people they know. Almost everybody knows somebody who's an expert at something.

Jesse, a college student in New York, decided in middle school that lacrosse was his favorite sport. "As far as mentors go," Jesse says, "there are always some players who have certain skills that you can try to add to your game. When I was younger, it was always some older player, but now I practice the moves of younger players, too."

In searching for a mentor, consider that you might eventually become one, too. Your experience will qualify you to guide others along their paths. To be a good mentor, all you have to do is respect the person you are guiding, listen to that person, and encourage your protégé along the way.

If you've ever watched *American Idol*, you know it takes courage for the contestants to audition and to allow themselves to be voted on or off the show. Every contestant has someone cheering them on; sometimes the best advice comes from the people you'd least expect, as the following profile demonstrates.

CLAY AIKEN

American Idol

"To me, singing is the single most joyous thing a person can do."

We all know how the world works. Nerdy kids who want to be teachers do not become superstars. They do not have fan clubs and websites devoted to them. Yet, this is exactly what happened for Clay Aiken on "American Idol" in 2003.

Clay Aiken was born Clayton Holmes Grissom on November 30, 1978, in Raleigh, North Carolina. From an early age, he loved music. His mother says people would give him a dollar to sing. Despite his love for music, Clay hadn't really considered it as a career.

As a child, Clay also loved helping young children. He wanted to be a school principal, and in December 2003 he graduated from the University of North Carolina–Charlotte with a special education degree. Clay cofounded the Buben-Aiken Foundation to help autistic children and individuals with other physical and mental disabilities. Clay still heads the foundation; he is also a UNICEF ambassador to bring attention to the plight of the world's children.

Clay has stated in interviews that he was never a popular kid on the block. He always felt "nerdy." While attending col-  lege, Clay worked with an autistic boy, Michael, whose mother suggested to Clay that he audition for "American Idol" in Atlanta. Clay was surprised when he made it through the first round of auditions. As he set out for Hollywood, it wasn't smooth sailing. He was kicked off the show, but he was later brought back as a wildcard. He didn't even win the actual competition. He took second place, but he was so impressive that he was offered a contract anyway.

He took the contract and hasn't looked back. Clay's debut solo CD, *Measure of a Man,* sold more than 612,000 copies the first week and more than 2.6 million overall, and it was certified Double Platinum. His list of musical accomplishments keeps growing. His book, *Learning to Sing: Hearing the Music in Your Life,* spent several weeks on the *New York Times* nonfiction best-seller list. He encourages readers, especially young people, to find what they love to do and be true to who they are. Clay's story is about being the underdog, the not-so-popular kid, the "nice guy" who finished first, even if he came in second.

Sources: Aiken, Clay. *Learning to Sing: Hearing the Music in Your Life.* Random House. 2004.

Clay's Foundation. http://thebubelaikenfoundation.com/

Crazy about Support Clay—Clay Maniacs www.claymaniacs.com/Bio.html

Fun Trivia www.funtrivia.com/en/Music/American-Idol-14740.html

IMDb Website: Clay Aiken www.imdb.com/name/nm1341750/bio

"Music News for You" Curlio.com www.curlio.com/spc_showarticle.php?id=1083&page=last (Curlio,1)

Profile Clues to Use

How did Clay Aiken develop his passion?

_____

_____

_____

_____

What are some obstacles he had to overcome?

_____

_____

_____

How do you see yourself as similar or dissimilar to him?

_____

_____

_____

_____

SELF-DISCOVERY QUESTIONS

What is one thing you'd love to have someone teach you?

_____

_____

Why would you like to learn it?

_____

_____

SELF-DISCOVERY ACTIVITY

Finding a mentor

Earlier in this chapter you read about Alyssa's mentor, who was a friend of the family. You can find mentors almost anywhere—in your school, your community, and even right in your own home. Here is a checklist for defining what you are looking for in a mentor:

- Write down what you expect from a mentor, keeping in mind what you need to reach your goals.

_____

_____

_____

- Make a list of people who you think would make an ideal mentor for you. Along with your personal goals, these people should have the capacity to care for you, respect you, and encourage you to continue toward whatever it is you want to achieve. You want to make sure you're following the right leader.

_____

_____

_____

_____

_____

- Choose three out of your list of possible mentors.

_____

_____

_____

- Plan a meeting with your possible mentor. Asking someone to meet with you can be as simple as offering to buy a soda. You can meet with the candidates in their offices, as well. Make sure you are respectful of your mentor's time. Bring your goal sheet with you so you can show your mentor what you are trying to achieve.

- Determine to be a good protégé. How can you get the most out of a mentoring relationship?

A leading expert on mentoring is Soren Gordhamer. Frustrated by the lack of mentorship in the United States, he decided to go on a quest to search for his own. He wanted to compile a series of interviews that would help teens and young adults become more focused and sure of themselves. After traveling the world and interviewing numerous leaders, environmentalists, psychologists, and great thinkers, Soren recorded the results of his research in a book titled *Meetings with Mentors*. You can check it out at your local library or through the interlibrary loan system.

Remember, wherever you are in life and whatever you are doing, your wings will require someone else's wind for you to soar.

slaying your
personal dragons

OVERCOMING OBSTACLES

*"Fear is that little darkroom where negatives
are developed."*

—MICHAEL PRITCHARD,
MOTIVATIONAL SPEAKER AND FACILITATOR

Live life obstacle free.

Obstacle *n.* that which stands in the way;
a hindrance or obstruction

Legend describes dragons as large lizardlike creatures
that breathe fire and have long, scaly tails. These mythical beasts
are often found in the folklore of many ancient European and
Asian cultures. In China, for instance, the traditional New Year's
Day parade includes a group of people who wind through city
streets wearing a large dragon costume to promote good luck and
wealth in the coming year.

Dragons can also symbolize intense human emotions like
anger, fear, and sadness. In this sense, we all have dragons since we
all experience these feelings. According to neuropsychologist Dr. L.
Michael Hall, "If we are pushed to our limits, a dragon just might
pop out. Some will roar. Others will whimper. Some will huff and
puff and rage and carry on in dramatic and melodramatic ways.
Others will just roll over and act dead."

In his book, *Dragon Slaying* (2000, Neuro-
Semantic Publications), Dr. Hall writes that the
problem with dragons is that they can undermine
our self-confidence and happiness. Therefore, he
says, we need "to tame, harness or transform
them so that we have more vitality for life."

navigating life's obstacles

Have you ever run an obstacle course? If
so, you know how different barriers can slow you down.
Some of these obstacles might be fun to go over and
around. Others, like having to grab a rope and climb over a wall,
take more effort.

If you let them, obstacles can create dragons in your life. An obstacle can be just about anything, but one thing that all obstacles have in common is that they tend to create a personal crisis. This crisis usually signals that something needs to change or that an adjustment needs to be made. Some people have great difficulty adjusting to life's problems and challenges. This often results in their gifts and talents lying **dormant** or being less fruitful within their lives. Obstacles can become either barriers to success or opportunities for personal growth. It's how you handle the obstacle that makes all the difference.

Dormant *adj.* asleep, inactive; not actively growing

Obstacles can also create a unique opportunity to grow. Obstacles can create what one author calls "a crisis of faith" because you must choose to either **focus** on the enormity of the obstacle and see it as immovable, or you can choose to focus on your own creativity to move through or around the obstacle.

In the whimsical story *Who Moved My Cheese?* a group of mice react in varying ways to a problem in their workplace. Overnight someone has moved their food supply. Their cheese is missing! One of the mice keeps going back to the same spot morning after morning looking for his cheese. When it doesn't reappear, he becomes discouraged. A few other mice become angry that their cheese has been moved, and they go on their way grumbling and complaining. Only one mouse accepts that the cheese has been moved and creatively figures out how to locate cheese someplace else.

Emily, a student in Orchard Lake, Michigan, says that she didn't know what she was capable of until she was forced to try new things. Emily explains:

> Ever since I was young, I've loved to draw and paint. I've taken a lot of art classes and art-related classes through school, such as drawing, studio survey, photography, and imaging on the computer. I also attended an extremely challenging fashion design class, and I loved

it. I'm continually working on projects around the house, too. I'm currently painting my bedroom closet with black and white diamonds, accented with gold. I also like to paint furniture with fun colors and unique designs.

The following is a profile of one person's determination to not give up in spite of many obstacles.

DR. BEN CARSON

Reaching higher

"I did not like school very much and there was no reason why I should. Inasmuch as I was the dumbest kid in the class, what did I have to look forward to?"

When his parents divorced, Ben Carson grew up trying to survive in his rough neighborhood of Detroit, Michigan. His mother, a single parent with only a third-grade education, raised two sons, Ben and his brother. Ben was an incredibly angry child with low self-esteem and lower grades. "The others laughed at me and made jokes about me every day. I really felt I was the stupidest kid in the fifth grade."

Although Ben's mother suffered all her life with mental illness (which doctors didn't know much about at the time), and she was in and out of psychiatric hospitals, she refused to give up on her children's future. When Ben was in the fifth grade, his mother made an important decision: Her sons' lives would revolve around education. She restricted their weekly television viewing to two shows. In addition, they were required to read and write two book reports each week.

As a fifth grader, Ben had never read an entire book. By sixth grade, because of obeying his mother's rules, he had become an avid reader. One day his teacher held up a rock and asked the class what a rock consisted of. Not even the smartest kids knew. Ben had read about rocks in one of his "assigned" books and was able to answer correctly. No one ever called him the stupidest kid in the class after that.

Ben continued to work extremely hard in school. He rose to the top of his high school class and earned a scholarship to Yale University. Later he studied neurosurgery (brain surgery) at the University of Michigan Medical School. He then went to work at Johns Hopkins University, one of the world's leading medical schools; there, at age 32, he became the youngest surgeon in the nation to hold the title of Director of Pediatric Surgery. Each year, Dr. Carson performs more than 500 surgeries on children who have brain tumors or other neurological conditions.

In spite of his incredibly busy schedule, Dr. Carson has dedicated himself to helping kids find their gifts and talents. He's written three books that have won numerous prestigious awards: *Gifted Hands, Think Big,* and *The Big Picture.* He also gives motivational talks to large groups of young people. He believes that the sky is the limit for everyone.

Sources: American Dreams. From Slow Learner to Brilliant Brain Surgeon, www.usdreams.com/Carson.html

Top Blacks: Positive Profiles of People of Color. Dr. Ben Carson, Director, Pediatric Neurosurgery, The Johns Hopkins, www.topblacks.com/medicine/ben-carson.htm

Profile Clues to Use

How did Ben Carson develop his abilities?

_____

_____

_____

_____

What are some obstacles he had to overcome?

_____

_____

_____

_____

How do you see yourself as similar or dissimilar to him?

_____

_____

_____

_____

You are what you think

As the profile story on Dr. Ben Carson points out, if left unchecked, negative thoughts about yourself can be an obstacle to success. As a child, Ben started out believing he was dumb. Thankfully, his mother helped him discard these self-doubts, and gradually he came to believe in himself.

You may not pay much attention to what you think about because thinking comes as naturally as breathing. But your thoughts, particularly when your mind is free to roam, can actually chart the course of your life by steering it in a particular direction, much like a steering wheel directs a car. That's why the most important conversation you can have is the one you have with yourself.

Healthy thoughts, those with a positive outlook, are capable of helping you move through or around obstacles and guiding you safely to your desired destination. Likewise, self-deprecating thoughts like "I'll never be any good at this," "I'm not pretty enough," "I'm too short," "I don't deserve good things to happen to me," and so on can **thwart** your opportunities to discover your true potential.

Thwart *tr.v.* to defeat the hopes or aspirations of

Although obstacles can block our gifts and talents, not every obstacle does. For example, a person can have a learning disability in math but may be talented in writing proposals for his company. In this case, the disability doesn't necessarily affect one's job performance.

Another example of an obstacle that interferes with talent is a lack of support, such as an individual whose family discourages him from investing time in his passion. Perhaps a child feels discouraged because the school she attends doesn't offer enrichment classes to help her excel in her talent for art.

fear factor

Fear can be a major obstacle to discovering and developing gifts and talents. Consider this true story about Samantha, an eighth grader in Los Angeles. One day Samantha heard an announcement over her school's loud speaker that a talent show was going to be held the following month in the school's auditorium. She smiled to herself as she began to think about her talents, but the smile quickly faded as she considered her options. She knew how to make delicious Spanish rice, but she couldn't bring her stove to school. She also was pretty good at teaching her dog tricks, but she knew he would freak out in front of a large audience.

There was one thing, though, that Samantha was really good at, but it was a hidden talent. Few people knew about it except her family and her martial arts instructor. Samantha had just earned her brown belt in karate. She had only one more level to go before receiving a black belt, which is the highest honor. "If I do karate for the talent show," Samantha thought to herself, "the kids might make fun of me." She was afraid the girls would call her a tomboy and that the boys would say they were better at karate than she was. Samantha swallowed hard while thinking about what might happen.

Why was Samantha afraid to showcase her talent? What do you think she should do? What would you tell her? Thankfully, Samantha overcame her fear and participated in the show. The students loved her karate performance and clapped wildly when she was done. In fact, her physical education teacher asked Samantha to give a few lessons in gym class.

Sometimes fears develop because of self-doubt. Fear can also create additional obstacles during life, not only causing a person to withdraw from his or her passion but also from other areas of interest. Fear can be overcome, but in order for this to happen you must face your fears. Like Samantha, you must take a risk. She didn't know for sure how the kids would react to her karate performance, but she did know that for her own sake, she couldn't let fear hold her back from showcasing her talent. What if the kids would have made fun of her?

As scary as it is to face your fears (like encountering a dragon), it is crucial to do so. Admitting you are fearful in a given moment gives you the power to do something about it. Successful people aren't those without fears, they are those who learn how "to tame, harness or transform them," to use Dr. Hall's words earlier in this chapter. Throughout this book you're reading about people who overcome all kinds of obstacles on the road to success, including fear. The following is another example.

ACTING OUT

Amelia, an intelligent and talented young woman, is creating a place for herself in the world of acting. Every morning when she wakes up, Amelia prepares herself for another busy day in New York City. Amelia is a recent graduate from the Tisch School of the Arts at New York University. She is passionate about her life as an actress simply because she is getting to do what she loves. Although her self-esteem and confidence are quite high today, at one time she suffered from self-doubt.

Amelia developed an interest in music when she was a toddler. Her father was very much involved in music and was constantly singing and playing music with her. At age five, Amelia took part in "Oliver," her first musical production. It was here that she discovered how strong her passion for music and theater truly was. At the time, Amelia did not realize that she would devote a great deal of her life to theater, yet she could sense how much she liked the experience. Amelia explains: "I knew that I was doing what I really enjoyed." These feelings inspired Amelia to pursue her interests in music and theater.

Throughout elementary, middle, and high school, Amelia's family supported her interests. Amelia studied numerous forms of dance, including tap, jazz, and lyrical. She studied voice and participated in many acting classes. She auditioned for musical after musical, and her talent landed her many major roles.

Despite her success, competition is often difficult for child actors, and at times Amelia felt intense self-doubt. If she did not get a part she had hoped for, she often questioned her abilities, thinking she might not be good enough. Amelia discovered ways that she could get through feelings of self-doubt: "Whenever I felt self-doubt I would go to the people who support me and believe in me."

As Amelia grew older, her passion for acting grew stronger. By the end of high school she decided that she wanted music and acting to form permanent places in her life. Some supported Amelia's decision to pursue a BFA in theater, while others discouraged it. Several people believed that acting was not a good path for her to travel, because a career in acting does not guarantee a good salary.

But Amelia knew that acting was what she wanted to pursue, so she did not let the negative comments discourage her. Instead, she spent four years working diligently at New York University, envisioning her future career in acting.

Today Amelia works in New York City as an actress. She constantly auditions and often lands roles. Sometimes she faces rejection, which is a common aspect of a career in acting. Regardless, Amelia learns something new at each audition. Her goal is to become a member of Equity, a highly competitive community of actors and actresses with Broadway status.

Experience, constant development, and growth are all essential in the world of acting. Although Amelia has already received formal education, she continues to study singing and acting. The process is ongoing: "You never stop learning, you're always growing."

The following profile gives an example of how inner motivation helped overcome gender bias.

DANICA PATRICK

Life in overdrive

"I was put here for one reason and that's to drive race cars."

Danica Patrick, of Beloit, Wisconsin, discovered her love of race-car driving almost by accident. At the age of 10, she wound up in a go-kart, going along for the ride because her younger sister, Brooke, had asked her parents to let her try racing. Brooke, now 20, quickly lost interest after crashing four times in one race. Danica, on the other hand, was hooked.

While successfully moving up the ladder of youth go-kart racing, she attracted the interest of racing officials who suggested she hone her skills. Danica realized that if she was really going to make a living by racing, she'd have to go to Great Britain—the center of open-wheel road racing—for an apprenticeship.

At the age of 16, Danica joined the European racing circuit and began training to become a world class racer. When asked about giving up normal teenage activities to race, she said, "In my eyes it wasn't really a sacrifice at all. I wasn't missing out; I was doing bigger and better things" ("Girl Vision," p. 122A).

From that start she worked her way back to the United States by teaming up with the Toyota Atlantic Championship and then  the Indy Racing League. Her commitment to racing, combined with her talent, is what attracted sponsors like Bobby Rahal, who put her in touch with Ford Motor Company. Rahal said, "It really impressed me that at such a young age she would leave home and go to live in England. That spoke volumes about her commitment. A lot of young people say they want to be race car drivers, but not many are willing to do the things you have to do."

Danica had many fans and admirers right from the start of her career; then, in 2005, she turned motor sports on its head by becoming the first woman ever to lead the field at the Indianapolis 500, and she earned the coveted title, "Indy Rookie of the Year." Former Indy 500 driver Sarah Fisher said, "When she wins, it will be good for all women who want to race."

Sources: Carney, Dan. *Profile: Danica Patrick: One of the Hottest New Driving Talents in America.* 2006. European Car. Accessed June 7, 2006. www.europeancarweb.com/features/0306ec_dpatrick

Danica Patrick. 2006. Chiff.com. Accessed June 7, 2006. www.chiff.com/recreation/sports/sports-stars/danica-patrick-2.htm

Danica Patrick. 2005. Sexy Danica Patrick. Accessed June 7, 2006. www.sexydanicapatrick.com/index.html

Girl Vision. 2005. *Chicago Sun-Times.* May 29, p. 122A.

Profile Clues to Use

How did Danica discover and develop her abilities?

_____

_____

_____

What are some obstacles she had to overcome?

_____

_____

_____

How do you see yourself as similar or dissimilar to her?

_____

_____

_____

_____

ife coaching*

You are no doubt familiar with coaching in athletics, but did you know that coaches can be found in other areas of life? For Danica Patrick, coaching came in the form of race car sponsors and former Indy drivers.

Many people today use coaching techniques to help them improve or achieve success in one or more areas of life. Life coaches can be specialists in various areas; there are dating coaches,

---

*Life Coaching The publisher of this book offers training and certification to become a LifeBound coach. Please visit our web site at www.lifebound.com for more information.

finance coaches, career coaches, education coaches, and parenting coaches, to name a few. These coaching experts help people achieve their life-improvement goals.

If you believe that fear or some other dragon is seriously holding you back from discovering or developing your gifts and talents, you may want to consider finding a mentor, professional counselor, or life coach. Of course, you should always talk with a parent or other trusted adult first. Sometimes the people who know you best are the ones who can help you the most.

SELF-DISCOVERY QUESTIONS

What obstacles have you encountered so far in your life?

_____

_____

What self-doubts or problems have arisen as a result of these obstacles?

_____

_____

_____

In what ways have these obstacles and self-doubts interfered with discovering or developing your gifts and talents?

_____

_____

_____

When was the last time you felt you failed at something?

_____

_____

How do you tend to handle failure or disappointment?

_____

_____

_____

What helps you or could help you manage these feelings better?

_____

_____

_____

SELF-DISCOVERY ACTIVITY

Interview a role model

While it's perfectly okay to have a famous role model in mind, for this exercise you should choose someone you know personally—someone who is accessible and is someone you admire and respect. Contact that person this week and ask about any fears or obstacles he or she overcame.

You may choose to interview your role model, and take notes, or you could record the responses on tape so you can play it back to yourself later, or you may simply listen and discuss your thoughts about what he or she has shared. Here are some questions you could ask. Feel free to come up with questions of your own!

1. What obstacles have you had to overcome in your life?

2. What and/or who helped you overcome these obstacles?

3. What is your best advice for me or for anyone else who wants to be successful?

7

developing
self-leadership

**UNDERSTANDING YOUR STRENGTHS
AND MANAGING YOUR WEAKNESSES**

*"Anyone who has never made a mistake
has never tried anything new."*

—ALBERT EINSTEIN

S E C R E T **7**

Create opportunities for yourself.

Strength *n.* a strong attribute or inherent asset

Trent, a fourth grader, wanted to play basketball competitively, but he was too young to try out for the school team and the leagues in his community were already full. One evening, while he and his dad were watching the local college team play, an idea popped into his head: "Maybe I could offer to be the water boy for the team." The team's coach (and Trent's dad) loved the idea. Trent spent the season passing out bottles of sports drink to the players. The coach also invited him into the locker room to hear the team plays. Trent was as close as possible to the sport he loved. He had created an opportunity for himself.

Michelle, a ninth grader, had an interest in fashion design but, other than looking at glossy magazines, she wasn't sure how to learn more about her interest. One day, while shopping with her friends at the mall, they entered a new clothing store. Michelle noticed that things looked a little untidy and a few unopened boxes were stacked on the counter. "What are those for?" Michelle asked the clerk as she pointed to the boxes. "Oh, those are filled with new sweaters for the season. I just haven't had time to organize everything," the clerk replied. "Would you like some free help?" Michelle asked. The clerk smiled.

Michelle began coming in on Saturday mornings to help out. Not only did she learn more about designer labels, she also learned about how to manage a store. Michelle is now a college senior majoring in fashion design. She already has a job with Saks Fifth Avenue upon graduation. Michelle created an opportunity for herself.

It's up to you

Ultimately, it's up to you to develop your abilities and interests. Some people are really good at one thing, but they don't know what their other gifts might be. Other people are good at several things but don't feel that they shine in any one area. When it comes to strengths, you may have several. People also have hidden talents that don't surface until they've tried something new.

Before you can know how to best use your strengths, you must know what they are. Everyone has at least one talent, and many people have multiple gifts. It is often those with multiple gifts who find themselves stuck! With so many choices and paths possible, multitalented people must be careful not to rest on their laurels or be held back in a maze of options. In the list below, mark the ones that you believe are your strengths.

○ Making others laugh or smile   ○ Designing

○ Creating something from nothing   ○ Serving others

○ Making people and things beautiful   ○ Communicating

○ Having a sense of style   ○ Entertaining

○ Comforting others   ○ Business sense

○ Inspiring or motivating others   ○ Writing

○ Mental intelligence   ○ Organizing

○ Emotional intelligence   ○ Leading

○ Physical stamina   ○ Teaching

○ Helping others   ○ Wisdom

○ Problem-solving   ○ Knowledge

○ Unique life experiences

The last item in the left column may surprise you: unique life experiences. Why consider "unique life experiences" a gift?

Throughout your life you may have gone through challenging or unique experiences, sometimes due to tragic circumstances. Important lessons can be learned from all of your experiences—from learning a foreign language to overcoming an addiction to surviving an illness or experiencing a loss. For example, if you were born in another country and you've had to adjust to life in the United States, that is a unique experience.

If you look at some of your unique life experiences as gifts that have helped shape you as a person—hopefully, as a better person—then you can open your eyes to ways of using such experiences in a positive way. Allow every experience to serve as a tool for personal growth, and you'll become stronger in character with each passing day.

It takes a lot of energy to succeed when your best gifts go underused or not used at all. When you are trying to move forward in life, it is critical to have the energy that comes from having a passion for what you are doing. Work you are passionate about takes less effort for you than it might for someone else, simply because it is work you are uniquely gifted to do.

be inspired

One of the best ways to discover and develop your strengths is to figure out what inspires you. Your inspiration might be an activity (like drawing), a person (such as your coach), or a place (like a music store). We've talked about the importance of role models and mentors in earlier chapters, and most people have at least one role model who inspires them. They look to this person to give them inspiration to try something new or to work harder. There are many other ways to gain inspiration:

- Listening to your favorite music
- Visiting an art gallery or museum
- Watching a live theater production
- Talking with a friend
- Reading about a great leader
- Taking a walk
- Watching a sunset
- Cooking or baking
- Browsing at your favorite store
- Exercising
- Laughing
- Writing a story or poem
- Making something with your hands
- Keeping a journal
- Drawing, painting, sculpting—anything that's creative!

african drumming

Nothing inspires Prince Bey more than African drumming, which he discovered as a child growing up on the west side of Chicago, an area of the city that is notorious for gangs. "When I was a boy, Martin Luther King Jr. was assassinated, and the race riots were raging. I took up African drumming as a way to stay connected to my heritage and to teach today's youth about our cultural roots." (Source: Personal communication.)

Bey performs at all types of events throughout the year, with a packed schedule in February during Black History month. "I play two drums simultaneously, but audiences have told me the beat is so powerful that it sounds like 20 drums."

At his performances, Bey wears traditional African clothing and usually has a professional narrator with him who connects the music to stories. For example, children always love Bey's performance of *Annszi the Spider*, an African folktale about a crafty black widow spider who shares her wisdom with friends.

The following is an inspiring profile of a scientist who uses his creativity to discover how plants in the rain forest can cure diseases.

ELOY RODRIGUEZ

"Medicine Man"

"Never let yourself be discouraged by negative and mean spirited people. Education will get you what you want in life, but you must work for it."

Eloy Rodriguez grew up in south Texas in one of the poorest counties in the United States. He grew up with 67 cousins, all living within a five-block radius. The family members supported one another, and 64 of his cousins received college degrees. It wasn't easy. Opportunities had to be created by hard work and common sense.

Eloy's first job was picking cotton as a migrant worker. This was how he discovered that he loved plants and was fascinated by the ecosystem. Counselors in high school pushed him to get vocational training to learn auto mechanics, but he hated fixing cars and decided to do something different. Later, he majored in accounting and discovered he didn't like that very much, either. Eloy got a job cleaning a laboratory, and it was then that he became interested in science. He decided to major in zoology and biochemistry at the University of Texas. He worked very hard and wrote 23 scholarly articles by the time he finished graduate school.

Eloy turned his interest to the rain forest and finding plants that can cure disease. He learned when animals are sick they can often cure themselves with plants. In the process, Eloy created an entirely new kind of science called *Zoopharmacognosy,* which is the study of how animals medicate themselves. He also was a consultant on a movie, *The Medicine Man,* about a scientist who works deep in the jungle studying plants and animals.

Eloy believes strongly in helping young people find their gifts and makes opportunities for them in his field. He works with students from all races and cultures. His lab is so diverse that it's often referred to as the "United Nations Laboratory." "I try to involve all of my students in the spirit of scientific discovery, which, for me, is the most exciting part of being a Chicano professor."

Eloy tells students that there will always be people who tell you that you can't do things. He stresses the importance of knowing how to read and write well and to think deeply about what you read. Who knows what future cures Eloy will discover deep in the jungle, all because he was determined to find what sparked his interest.

Sources: *Eloy Rodriguez, Natural Products Chemist.* 2006. Society for Advancement of Chicanos and Native Americans in Science. Accessed June 7, 2006. www.cowz.com/sacnas/bio/rodrighig.html

Profile Clues to Use

How did Eloy Rodriguez develop his abilities?

What are some obstacles he faced?

_____

_____

_____

_____

How do you see yourself as similar or dissimilar to him?

_____

_____

_____

_____

environment

The type of environment you enjoy being in is another important clue to your strengths. Eloy Rodriguez, for example, thrives in the rain forest and in a laboratory. Some people prefer activities that are predictable and involve a level of repetition rather than surprises. Others are multitaskers; they love to do several things at once and enjoy tackling anything new.

The story of two Daves, and a story of Emily

This is a story about two best friends who are both named Dave. They each chose a working environment that enhances who they are. Dave One is a college student. He likes to study and work on hobbies in a cool, well-lit, quiet room. He doesn't focus very well if the radio or TV is on or if there are other distractions. He occasionally works with one other student to study for math tests, but mostly he works by himself.

Dave Two works in a coffee shop. He takes customer orders, makes coffee, talks to customers, and does many tasks at once. He works at a fast pace and loves it. All of the activity that's always going on around him makes him feel energized. You can see how two people who have similar interests and are great friends can have very different learning and working styles.

Emily is another example. She loves being outside, and she has a passion for horses. When she was five years old, Emily admired them and felt inspired whenever she watched her older sister ride. Today, as a seventeen-year-old, Emily is a stellar rider and knows how to care for horses. Last year Emily got an equine friend all her own, Scooby, a nine-year-old quarter horse.

From the beginning of her riding experience, Emily studied a challenging riding style called English riding. She took lessons one to two times a week, but Emily found herself longing for more practice. As years passed, Emily excelled in riding and wanted to challenge herself. In seventh grade, with hopes of finding this challenge, she decided to switch barns. Her family supported her decision, and her mother searched online for a place where she could continue riding. Emily decided to begin training at the King Oak Farm.

The King Oak Farm fulfilled Emily's needs. Here, the riding was more disciplined and complex, and the level of competition was higher. Because Emily felt satisfied, she decided to stay at the King Oak Farm; she still trains there today. Emily spends a great deal of her life at the barn; during the school year she rides six days a week. She arrives at the barn at around 2:30 P.M., right after classes end, and spends several hours riding and caring for the horses. Emily spends her weekends at the barn, and during the summer she goes there every day.

Clearly, Emily's passion is time consuming. She has learned that sacrifice is necessary if she wants to devote so much time to horses. She explains: "It's a lot more time consuming than people think. There's always more to learn and more to do. You have to give some things up. I had to stop playing other sports because I didn't have enough time. But I'm happy about my decisions."

With high school graduation around the corner, Emily must consider her future ambitions. She is thinking about becoming a veterinarian, and she also wants to pursue the idea of owning or managing a barn. Either way, Emily has loved her experience with horses and plans on keeping them in her life.

The following is a profile on one of our nation's leaders, who thrives in a political environment. As you're reading, think about how his story ties in with the title of this chapter, "Developing Self-Leadership," and be sure to answer the questions at the end of the profile.

BARACK OBAMA

Leading by example

"[My parents] imagined me going to the best schools in the land, even though they weren't rich, because in a generous America you don't have to be rich to achieve your potential."

Barack Obama was born in Honolulu, Hawaii, in 1961, to an American mother and a Kenyan father. His early years were marked by upheaval. When he was two years old his parents divorced, and his father moved back to Kenya, in Africa. Barack and his mother remained in Hawaii. From the time he was six until he was ten, after his mother remarried, the family lived in Jakarta, Indonesia—a lush and beautiful yet profoundly poor country. Barack experienced the harsh realities of life in a developing country.

Eventually, Barack's family returned to the States, and he graduated from school in Hawaii. Those years were confusing and often difficult. He was raised primarily by his grandparents, who were white; while his father wrote to him often, Barack saw his father only once, when he was ten. In his book *Dreams from My Father,* Barack talks about being a teenager and feeling lost. He tells how he went to Kenya as an adult to meet his father's family and to learn about that part of his heritage.

Barack attended Columbia University in New York and dealt with "inescapable racial tension." When he graduated, he moved to Chicago where he became a community organizer in the city's south side. Three years later, he was accepted to Harvard Law School. His brilliance and hard work paid off. In 1990, Barack became the first African American president of the *Harvard Law Review.*

His career headed straight up. He was offered a position as a clerk for the chief judge of the United States Court of Appeals for the DC circuit. The position was one of the most prestigious jobs that could be offered to a law student. Barack turned it down. Instead, he went back to Chicago to practice civil-rights law, representing victims of housing and employment discrimination. He also began teaching at the University of Chicago Law School.

In 2004, Barack became the fifth African American to serve in the Senate and the only African American in the Senate at that time. His political style is strong, intelligent, and compelling, and he has earned the respect of opponents and critics alike. Many people consider him a future presidential candidate.

Finnegan, William. *How the son of a Kenyan economist became an Illinois Everyman.* The New Yorker Issue of 2004-05-31 Posted 2004-05-24. www.newyorker.com/fact/content/?040531fa_fact1

Infoplease: Barack Obama. www.infoplease.com/ipa/A0930136.html

---

Profile Clues to Use

How did Barack Obama develop his abilities?

_____

_____

_____

What are some obstacles he faced?

_____

_____

_____

How do you see yourself as similar or dissimilar to him?

_____

_____

_____

Weak spots

Weakness *n.* a defect in character or ability; a physical or intellectual imperfection or impairment

Weaknesses are the opposite of strengths. They are things you may feel you're not good at. You may even be embarrassed by your weak spots. Many people try to hide their weaknesses. Why do you think it's hard for people to admit or work on their weaknesses? Some of the teens we interviewed had this to say:

> "Because no one likes to think about what they're not good at."

> "Some people don't want to improve."

> "It's hard to know what would help."

No matter what your weaknesses may be, don't let them define who you are. Below is a poem about not allowing test scores to become your identity. The meaning of this poem could apply to just about any weakness a person may have.

I'M NOT A TEST SCORE!

I am not a test score . . .
an average, a calculation, or percentile;
nor a school's grade or security blanket,
'cause my Mama said I'm a precious child.

I'm a living, breathing, walking miracle,
and sometimes, yes, a little easy to ignore;
but one thing I do know for sure,
I'm not just a test score.

See, I'm not a basic skill to be measured,
standardized or compared on a chart,
I possess the promise of what's possible,
I'm a priceless work of art.

I'll admit, I can be spoiled at times,
always asking and expecting more,
but you told me, if I believe it, I can achieve it,
so there's no way I can be a test score.

So don't analyze or judge me,
'cause like you, I smile too when I see the sun,
and like you, my soul longs to be embraced,
and to be respected by everyone.

I know I talk too much and "get on your last nerve,"
'cause sometimes school can feel like a chore;
but what else would you expect from me
when all you do is treat me like a test score?

So I will tell you today, tomorrow,
and each day until the end of the year,
"go ahead and test me and score me,"
but I won't allow it reduce me to tears.

See, I'm going to love myself,
and see myself through my eyes . . . not yours;
because in the end,
what you think of me is none of my business,
'cause I know . . . I'm more than a test score.

© by Joe A. Martin, Jr., 1-888-576-2377 www.ProfessorMartin.com

S eeking help

If you feel your weakness is holding you back, take heart. There are ways to compensate for a weak spot, and many people who can help you. You just need to take the first step by seeking the right kind of help.

In order to manage your weakness so it doesn't become a **liability,** think about specific things you can do to improve. If you know you're not good in a subject in school, such as math, what are some things you can do to improve on that weakness? Here are a few ideas:

- Get a tutor
- Put more time into studying
- Ask your teacher to explain the lesson in a different way
- Ask your teacher for a practice test
- Study with someone who's good at math
- Improve your overall study skills

Liability *n.* something that acts as a disadvantage; drawback

O vercoming intense shyness

Many teenagers tell us that one problem they have is being shy. They'd like to feel less self-conscious and more comfortable about meeting new people. Sarah, a tenth grader, suffered from social phobia, which caused her to avoid being around groups of people, and she didn't know what to do about it. When surrounded by new faces, Sarah's anxiety overpowered her, and she felt like "a tiny mouse, cornered and frightened." All she wanted to do was run and hide, or become a fly on the wall. She rarely gave others the chance to get to know her. Sarah understood how important social skills are in life, and she knew they would become more essential as she grew older and ventured out into the world.

Sarah's eyes were opened when she sought help from a reputable counselor. She discovered the ways that some of her past experiences were now fueling her anxieties. As a shy child, Sarah's behavior was often considered "cute" by others. Realizing that she was shy, and not wanting to make her feel uncomfortable, many friends and family members refrained from expecting her to step forward.

To Sarah's surprise, within a relatively short period of time social interaction became much easier for her. She no longer felt withdrawn and no longer wanted to hide. Instead, Sarah now enjoys meeting and getting to know new people. Sarah has learned to manage her weakness.

SELF-DISCOVERY QUESTIONS

What is a weakness you think you have?

_____

_____

What makes it troublesome for you?

_____

_____

_____

_____

Has this weakness held you back from doing something you wanted to do?

_____

_____

_____

_____

How might you be able to compensate for this weakness?

_____

_____

_____

_____

What or who could help you improve in this area?

_____

_____

try a talent

We often take for granted many of the things we are able to do. These abilities, and our enjoyment or lack of enjoyment in doing them, can give additional clues to discovering strengths. Below is list of things you could do on your own. Try one each day for a month and see what you like best. Some activities, such as building a birdhouse, might require more than a day; you'll want to allow extra time for those.

- Brush a dog
- Fly a kite
- Create some origami (Japanese paper folding)

- Attend a festival or convention related to your interest
- Build something (e.g., a birdhouse, a K'NEX building kit, a model car)
- Cook or bake
- Listen to a friend
- Do a crossword puzzle
- Work on a jigsaw puzzle
- Learn and play a board game
- Play Sudoku (Japanese number puzzle)
- Read the Sunday comics
- Draw a comic strip
- Tell a joke
- Write a song
- Make up a dance
- Make up your own joke
- Make and send a card
- Write and send a letter
- Take a photograph
- Play an instrument
- Draw a picture
- Plant a flower
- Water a plant
- Sing a song
- Read a book
- Decorate your room
- Read to an elderly person
- Take part in a talent show
- Help a child with homework
- Teach someone how to do something

SELF-DISCOVERY ACTIVITY

Gift Game

Please complete the following activity.

The Gift Game*

Next to each GIFT listed, write down one of the following numbers in EACH box (to the left of it):

1	2	3
"That's definitely ME!"	"I'm NOT SURE that's me."	"That's definitely NOT me!"

Bring out potential	Start things	Explore the way	Empower others
Sell intangibles	Manage things	Persuade people	Make deals
Open doors	Analyze information	Discover resources	Translate things
See possibilities	Research things	Design things	Advance ideas
Make connections	Investigate things	Process things	Operate things
Straighten things up	Do the numbers	Organize things	See the big picture
Build things	Make things work	Shape environments	Fix things
Grow things	Solve problems	Resolve disputes	Get others to participate
Create trust	Build relationships	Heal wounds	Instruct people
Create dialogue	Give care	Facilitate change	Create things

* © RealWorld Student Success Course.

☐ Bring joy to others	☐ Awaken people's spirit	☐ Add humor	☐ Write things
☐ Compose themes	☐ Use body to have fun	☐ Perform events	☐ Break molds
☐ Get to the heart of matters	☐ Put the pieces together	☐ Help others overcome obstacles	☐ Make sure things are right

For every GIFT you put a **"1"** next to, write it down in the column below titled **"That's Definitely Me."**

Then continue by filling in the rest of the columns by answering the three remaining questions.

(1) That's Definitely Me	(2) What do I usually GIVE the most? (from #1 at left)	(3) What would OTHERS say I GIVE the most? (from #2)
(1)	(1)	(1)
(2)	(2)	(2)
(3)	(3)	(3)
(4)	(4)	(4)
(5)	(5)	(5)
(6)	(6)	What do I get most EXCITED about GIVING to others? (from #3 above)
(7)	(7)	
(8)	(8)	(1)
(9)	(9)	(2)
(10)	(10)	(3)
(11)		(4) WHO do I WANT to GIVE my gift to the most?
(12)		
(13)		(1)
(14)		(2)
(15)		(3)

Your Life's Objective: Once you've identified your GIFT(s) (using your heart, not your head), and you've decided WHO you want to give your gift to the most, the rest is quite simple. Find the type of work (not job) that will give you the best opportunity to share your GIFT(s) with the type of people (or things) who you most desire to work with and for.

Used with permission of Professor Joe Martin, www.RWuniversity.com, (850) 212-0227.

having an indomitable spirit

BEING YOUR BEST NOW AND IN THE FUTURE

"If a man is called to be a streetsweeper, he should sweep streets even as Michelangelo painted, or Beethoven composed music, or Shakespeare wrote poetry. He should sweep streets so well that all the hosts of heaven and earth will pause to say, here lived a great streetsweeper who did his job well."

—DR. MARTIN LUTHER KING, JR.

S E C R E T   8

Use your gifts and talents to fulfill a greater purpose.

Indomitable *adj.* not to be subdued

Success rarely comes easily. The most successful people aren't those without problems, nor has everything gone their way. You've read about some of them in your history books. You've studied great leaders and seen what they were up against. Often they were faced with terrifying, seemingly insurmountable difficulties. Yet they pushed forward in spite of their fears, which is why we admire them so much. Against all odds, they managed to achieve amazing feats. Consider the following teen whose brother's tragedy propelled her to develop a passion for fashion.

AN INSPIRATION FOR FASHION
by Katherine of Illinois

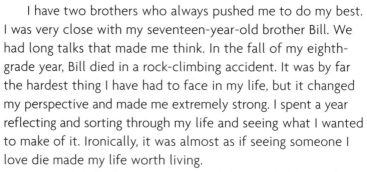

The one thing I enjoy most in life, besides family and friends, is fashion. Most girls will tell you they like fashion and shopping, but my liking for it goes far beyond. I love to learn about where garments come from, the marketing stand point, designer's inspirations, and the way a good outfit can boost a person's self esteem.

I have two brothers who always pushed me to do my best. I was very close with my seventeen-year-old brother Bill. We had long talks that made me think. In the fall of my eighth-grade year, Bill died in a rock-climbing accident. It was by far the hardest thing I have had to face in my life, but it changed my perspective and made me extremely strong. I spent a year reflecting and sorting through my life and seeing what I wanted to make of it. Ironically, it was almost as if seeing someone I love die made my life worth living.

I started designing clothes in the eighth grade. I learned everything I needed to know about making a garment. That year I made lots of clothes and sold them to kids at my school. My brother John encouraged me to pursue my dream of starting a fashion show. I became involved with a club called Room to Read, which sponsors education for children in developing countries. In May of my freshman year, I produced and ran the first Room to Read Fashion Show to raise money for the organization. We've raised more than $20,000! I continue presenting the fashion show every year, and each year it keeps getting better and better.

I'm a senior now, and in the past three years I have started a fashion show with growing success, designed clothing and sold it, been a part of Ford Models (I was in New York visiting my brother and got scouted in a shoe store), and am now on the fashion board at Nordstroms. I've also worked at a high-end boutique in my home town for the last year and half, which has been an incredible experience. With each new opportunity, I learn more and more about the fashion world, and I want nothing more than to be successful in my future career.

I have accomplished a lot in high school, and not just in my pursuit of fashion. Because of my brother's influence and death, I have discovered myself. I am proud to say that I am a very spiritual person, have developed great friendships, have learned to love my family, and realized that I am not going anywhere without their support. More important, I have learned to love my life no matter what the situation is and to go for it. I witnessed a life that was taken too early. My brother was a seventeen year old who experienced more in his life than most people in their eighties have experienced. If I can show the world a quarter of the inspiration my brother showed me, I will be a success.

great expectations

In this story, Katherine didn't expect the tragic loss of her brother, yet when he died she allowed the experience to shape her life for the good. We all expect certain things to happen in our lives. We may expect to do well in school, have a cute boyfriend or girlfriend, and have fun on the weekends. Some of us may have dreamy expectations of a good life, and we have well-visualized goals about how to achieve our heart's desires, while others may just aim to get through the day, with little thought of tomorrow or the future.

Regardless of our approach to life, there's one thing we can be sure of: We will face the unexpected. You may have heard the expression "Life is what happens when you're making other plans." How we deal with the unexpected comes from a sense of who we are, what we believe, and how well we adjust to the changes that come our way.

SELF-DISCOVERY QUESTIONS

What obstacle or difficulty do you have in your life?

_____

What are you doing to cope with this problem or issue?

_____

_____

_____

Are you coping in healthy or unhealthy ways?

_____

_____

What has happened that you weren't expecting?

_____

How did you handle this situation or issue?

_____

_____

The following profile shows how one special athlete did the unexpected by leading the way for other people to be generous.

JOEY CHEEK

Gold medalist

"I knew I had a very brief moment to do something substantial. . . . Rather than letting them get their traditional Olympic story about a kid from North Carolina who becomes a winter athlete, I was going to take over the story a bit."

Joey Cheek was born June 22, 1979, in Greensboro, North Carolina.

Cheek started his athletic career in his native North Carolina as a competitive inline skater. But then he watched Norwegian superstar Johann Olav Koss win three gold medals in the 1994 Olympic Games. That inspired him to switch to speed skating.

Because he couldn't train year-round in North Carolina, at 16 he moved to Canada by himself. For the next 10 years, he trained in Calgary, Alberta, to become World and Olympic Champion.

"Watching him [Koss] skate, he was the guy I wanted to be like," Cheek said. "At the time I had no idea that one day I would go on to win a gold medal, and I would be able to donate money to his organization." *(Person of the Week: Joey Cheek)*

That's exactly what he did. In the 2006 Winter Olympics at Torino, Italy, Joey won Gold in the 500 meters and Silver in the 1,000 meters. Olympians are awarded cash prizes for medals, and Joey won a total of $40,000. He stunned fans when he announced that he was donating all of his prize money to Koss' Right to Play charitable organization.

Joey wanted to use his success to help other people. This incredibly generous and touching move snowballed. He challenged companies to do more to help kids, and matching donations flooded in from around the globe. So many donations were offered that Joey started two of his own organizations: the Joey Cheek Charitable Fund and a Greensboro College scholarship. By the end of March 2006, more than $500,000 had been raised from his efforts and the support of his fans.

Joey's Olympic experience was far from over when his last race ended. As a result of the manner in which Joey Cheek conducted himself over the course of the seventeen days of the Olympic Games he was bestowed the greatest honor an Olympian can receive. He was elected by his athlete peers to carry the American flag into the closing ceremonies.

Joey knew about his gifts in skating from the time he was young. He knew he had what it takes to work hard and be a competitor. He also knew what kind of person he wanted to be, and he wanted to contribute to his world. But even he couldn't have known that his personality and his story would inspire so many other people to do so much.

Joey sums it up best on his website: "I am so grateful for all of the support I have gotten over the years. The media attention . . . has been pretty incredible, so it has really helped me promote *Right To Play*" (www.joeycheek.com).

Sources: *Another Olympic medal for Joey Cheek Helps to Raise US $300,000.* 2006. Right to Play. Accessed June 7, 2006. www.righttoplay.com/site/PageServer?pagename=news_torino_joeycheek_secondwin_feb2006

Jansen, Dan. *Joey Cheek: The Speedskater with a Heart of Gold.* 30 April 2006. Q Sports International. Accessed June 7, 2006. www.qsports.net/new2.html

Olympic Gold. 20 Feb 2006. JoeyCheek.com. Accessed June 7, 2006. www.joeycheek.com

Person of the Week: Joey Cheek. Olympic Speed Skater Became the Best in the World, Decided He Could Do Better. 24 Feb. 2006. ABC News. Accessed June 7, 2006. http://abcnews.go.com/WNT/PersonOfWeek/story?id=1659095&page=1

Profile Clues to Use

How did Joey Cheek develop his abilities?

What are some obstacles he faced?

_____

_____

_____

_____

_____

How do you see yourself as similar or dissimilar to him?

_____

_____

_____

_____

_____

learning to lead

In the previous chapter, we talked about self-leadership as a way to develop your strengths by seizing opportunities. In this chapter, we want to look at leadership in a broader sense because there are many ways to be a leader—for example, you can lead by your ideas, you can lead by helping others (as exemplified by this chapter's profile story on Joey Cheek), and you can lead by simply doing what needs to be done.

Some people are natural born leaders; they tend to take charge in every situation. Other people are situational leaders; they're good at leading on a specific project (say, building your school's float for the homecoming parade or being the captain of a team).

Leadership styles may also differ. Some lead quietly by example, while others are more exuberant, expressive leaders.

Your style of leadership doesn't matter as long as you feel comfortable with it. One of the marks of a great leader is the desire to take **initiative** and do what needs to be done in any given moment or situation.

Initiative *n.* a first move; the starting points of a process

S tarter kit for leaders

What are some ways you can develop yourself as a leader? Here are a few ideas to jump-start the process:

- **Take initiative at home.** Ask your parents if they need help with something; look around your house and in your yard and see what needs to be done. Don't always wait for someone to tell you what to do.

- **Accept a leadership role at school.** Run for student council or a class office, or try out as the captain of your team. If you don't get elected, offer to help the leader and learn from what you observe.

- **Look for opportunities in your neighborhood or community.** Rake leaves for the parks department, volunteer to be a summer camp counselor, tutor a child, help out at the library book fair, or deliver groceries to an elderly neighbor.

We are tempted to think that being a leader is like being a boss. You get to tell others what to do. In reality, the best leaders are those who seek to serve others. You'll see this as you grow up and watch other people in leadership positions. Great leaders are servant-leaders. The following profile story is the epitome of possessing the indomitable spirit of a true servant-leader.

WILMA MANKILLER

Cherokee Pride

"The only thing people wanted to talk about in 1983 was my being a woman. That was the most hurtful experience I've ever been through."

Wilma Mankiller was born in 1945 in the Cherokee Nation of Oklahoma. In 1993, she presented a moving speech recounting her efforts to rebuild the Cherokee Nation. You can read her speech at the web link http://gos.sbc.edu/m/mankiller.html.

Mankiller's passionate struggle to create a sustainable community among the Cherokee Nation and other Native Americans (when so many families, including her own, felt more like refugees than U. S. citizens), led her to become the first female Chief of the Cherokee Nation. She was also the first female in modern history to lead any Native American tribe. Before Wilma Mankiller came along, Cherokee girls did not think it was possible for a woman to be chief.

In a tribal election in 1983, Mankiller ran as deputy chief against Ross Swimmer, the incumbent principal chief. The two were elected. Swimmer resigned during his term, and Mankiller became acting chief. When her term was up she ran as chief herself. Many people opposed the idea of a woman chief; she received death threats during the campaign, and her car tires were slashed.

Things are very different now. Over time she won the respect of her people because of her impact on helping the Cherokee Nation achieve autonomy. Like many great leaders, Mankiller has faced personal tragedies of her own.

In 1979, she was in a car accident in which one of her best friends died and she almost lost her leg; she later had to undergo

17 operations. A year later she was diagnosed with myasthenia gravis, a chronic autoimmune disease that results in progressive skeletal muscle weakness. She has also undergone a kidney transplant. Instead of being bitter, however, Mankiller views her physical trauma as a realization of how fragile life is, and it has motivated her to continue serving her community. Her illness made it necessary for her to step down as chief, but she remains an inspiring force for women, not only for Native Americans, but for anyone who knows her story.

Sources: Mankiller, Wilma. Former Chief of the Cherokee Nation. *Rebuilding the Cherokee Nation,* speech at Sweet Briar College. April 2, 1993. Gifts of Speech. Accessed June 7, 2006. http://gos.sbc.edu/m/mankiller.html

Wilma Mankiller: Former Principal Chief of the Cherokee Nation. 2006. Powersource. Accessed June 7, 2006. www.powersource.com/gallery/people/wilma.html

Profile Clues to Use

How did Wilma Mankiller develop her abilities? (Visit the web link http://gos.sbc.edu/m/mankiller.html and read her speech for clues.)

_____

_____

_____

_____

_____

What are some obstacles she faced?

_____

_____

_____

_____

_____

How do you see yourself as similar or dissimilar to her?

_____

_____

_____

_____

_____

a nyone want to be mayor?

According to an article in *USA Today* (November 10, 2005), eighteen-year-old Michael Sessions has always been interested in politics, but it still came as a surprise to him when he won the mayoral election in his hometown of Hillsdale, Michigan, in 2005. He ran for office as a write-in candidate because he wasn't even old enough to vote when the ballots were first printed.

Sessions credits his success to careful research of the issues facing his community and to his parents, high school, and the many townspeople who supported him. He's also in the process of setting up a board of directors to help him make important decisions.

Sessions said he funded his campaign with the $700 he made from a summer job, and he planned to use his bedroom for an office.

g aining support

As the story about Michael Sessions illustrates, being a leader involves gaining support from other people. Isolation is a sure path to failure; all great leaders have a supporting cast. Keep in mind, too, that being a leader can be tough. There's often more pressure on you to perform; if you make a mistake, the consequences can affect people other than yourself. You want to take seriously any leadership role you have. People are looking to you to set an example. Yet the flip side is also true—all leaders need someone to lean on.

You can create a supportive circle of family and friends by extending friendship and support to them. Having caring, supportive people around you provides a huge boost during difficult times and makes the good times more fun. If you're facing a huge problem, however, you may need professional help. Don't be afraid to ask for what you need. Avoid thinking, "This problem will go away if I just ignore it." Most problems don't disappear on their own. We need each other.

Sadly, many teens grow up in homes where they aren't supported. Perhaps their parents have so many problems of their own that they do a poor job taking care of their kids. If this describes your situation, seek support from other adults and friends.

There are lots of people who want to help you. You need to reach out by simply saying, "I need to talk" or "I have this problem. Can you help me?" Talk to a teacher, a neighbor, a coach, or other trusted adult or friend. Don't face it alone. You deserve to be loved and to feel cared for.

Even if you aren't up against a huge problem, everyone gets in a slump once in a while. Friends can help pull you up and motivate you to keep going. Many leaders also run into great opposition, as the profile of Wilma Mankiller illustrates. Yet, in time, as the leaders demonstrate courage and good judgment, they can gain the support needed to make a difference in other people's lives.

SELF-DISCOVERY ACTIVITY

Self portrait

Wilma Mankiller is an example of someone who used her gifts and talents to promote justice among her tribe. Write a story about yourself, but from someone else's perspective (i.e., a parent, friend, teacher, pet, etc.). Here are some questions to consider:

- How would they describe you?
- What kind of person would they say you are?
- What kind of profession would they picture you doing in the future?

The story should describe you in as much detail as possible, everything from physical characteristics to personality to deep feelings. The story should have a plot, so your character should deal with and resolve some type of conflict (it can be fighting pirates or dealing with a friend; be as creative as you want). The point of the story is to illustrate your true character, your gifts and talents, and even your weaknesses.

SELF-DISCOVERY ACTIVITY

Make a collage

Cut out pictures from magazines—articles or advertisements—or use poems or any other images that inspire you to create a visual display of your dreams.

being true to yourself

DEVELOPING YOUR INSTINCTS

"Figure out who you are before the world starts telling you who you should be."

—DR. PHIL MCGRAW

"My parents embraced who I am. They didn't try to beat the tomboy out of me."

—ANN BANCROFT, POLAR EXPLORER

S E C R E T | **9**

Don't let the world squeeze you into its mold.

Instinct *n.* a natural or inherent aptitude, impulse, or capacity

marketing *versus who you are*

We live in a commercial world that is constantly trying to make a buck. Everything around you is designed to make you want to buy something. You are bombarded with advertising from internet, television, movies, magazines, the mall, stores, billboards, and pretty much any place else you might go. All of these things are telling you their products will do something for you. They might make you prettier, smarter, cooler, faster . . . well, you know the routine.

What does this have to do with your gifts and talents? The problem with living in a commercial world is that in this type of environment, marketers are sending you two messages: (1) you aren't good enough the way you are, and (2) if you become something else (preferably by buying our stuff) you'll be happier. In small doses, this might not be important. But you don't get it in small doses. You are told, many times a day, that there is an infinite list of things you should be. Unfortunately, people who follow these gimmicks and buy into the hype are rarely happy. They haven't found out who they are, what they're good at, or what's truly best for them. Despite what the ads tell you, none of the "right" products will make you happy or fulfilled if you're not using your strengths and engaging your interests.

As you've read in this book, successful people come from all types of backgrounds and face all sorts of challenges. Some of them had wonderful and supportive parents. Others had parents who were opposed to the directions they took. They

all had people along the way who told them that they couldn't
do it.

fish out of water

You may be struggling in an environment that tells you that being smart isn't
cool, but you love calculus. You're like a
fish out of water. You may be really good at playing video games
but have parents who think you're just not smart enough in
school. Your friends might be good at sports, and you're good at
board games like Monopoly. You may even be one of the many
people who feel like your gifts are a little dumb and won't serve
any real purpose.

Your parents, friends, teachers, and other people close to you
probably have a lot of expectations for you. Sometimes, these
expectations are based on things you liked when you were little
or on what other people would like for you. Sometimes, other
people have few or no expectations for you, and this also is hurtful. Whatever your situation and pressures you face, realize that
you're not alone. Others, including many of the people profiled
in this book, learned who they are in spite of expectations that
didn't match their personality.

For instance, Carson, a high school student in Tucson, Arizona, describes how following his instincts led him to one of the
greatest experiences of his life so far. He explains:

> As the end of my freshman year came around, we were obliged to
> fill out our class choices for the next school year. I had always been
> interested, since I had entered high school, in being on the staff of
> the school news magazine, *The Crusader*. I filled out my class-choic-
> es list and reviewed it with my parents. They were highly skeptical
> and discouraged me from taking the class, saying that it was a career
> I should never seek to go into, they themselves being journalists.
> I argued that it had always interested me, and besides it was high
> school, it wasn't life changing, and I needed something to do.

Newspaper journalism may not be the career I go into—in fact, I hope it is not—but it has been life changing. I decided that even though it was my first year, I was interested in business, marketing, and sales. I signed up for the editorial position of business manager. I soon came to realize that the newspaper took a huge amount of time, but the sense of accomplishment that I felt as I walked the halls and saw students reading the paper was incredible.

Teachers, students, and my parents would say things like, "It's ridiculous how much time you spend there." I thought about those arguments, but in the end I decided it was something I really loved, and I wasn't going to give it up. I am glad I made that decision, because after the first issues were completed and everyone got into the swing of things, our quality got steadily better and we got to know each other. I have made my best friends in that wonderful dump we affectionately call PUB [Publications]. I have never laughed so much or made so many friends in one place as in that room.

I had no idea how much I didn't know until I came into that room, and was surrounded by people with far more experience and talent. I learn new things literally every day in PUB. This experience has taught me to interact with as many people as you can, because you have no idea how much you can learn from other people.

Just because a person does not possess a certain talent for something does not mean you should cast them aside as worthless; you should instead look to their other attributes. There were people on the staff who were not good at writing or designing, but despite that they added to the quality of the staff. Just having an extra personality made the long slogs of production easier on myself and my fellow newspaper staff members. Putting out one of the highest-ranking high school papers in the United States is quite an accomplishment, but a greater accomplishment to me was that we made a big, highly dysfunctional, happy family.

As Carson's story illustrates, your gifts and talents underlie your skills, and they develop and evolve as you grow. If you're willing to keep working on them and finding new things to do, you'll learn that you have other gifts. You will also learn the best ways to use those gifts. Someone who is a great dancer may not necessarily enjoy teaching dance, even though that seems like a logical extension of the skill. You may also find that what makes you good at Monopoly helps you in business or with other issues. The following profile story shows how one man's instincts led him to create a multi–billion dollar empire from a coffee bean.

HOWARD SCHULTZ

Soul purpose

"I wanted to build a company with soul."

In 1971, the very first Starbucks opened in Seattle, selling only coffee beans in the beginning. Little did the founders know that ten years later, they would meet a man capable of turning that one coffee shop into a multi–billion dollar corporation. Howard Schultz learned about Starbucks when he worked for a company that sold coffeemakers to them. In 1981, Howard visited the store and fell in love with the company. He loved the care that the owners put into choosing their coffee beans and their dedication to educating the public about coffee.

Schultz decided he wanted to work for Starbucks, but the Starbucks owners didn't think they wanted Howard. He spent a year working to convince them to hire him. They finally hired him and made him the director of marketing and operations. Howard was inspired by stores in Italy that sold espresso and other brewed coffee, and he was convinced a similar concept could be successful in the United States. Starbucks' owners disagreed. Howard was so frustrated by their attitude that he quit and opened his own coffee-bar business.

His business was so successful that in one year he had enough money to buy Starbucks for $3.8 million. Starbucks' popularity increased during the 1990s, and the company began making a lot of money. Schultz wasn't willing to settle for being another rich CEO at the expense of his employees. He instituted business practices that took care of his employees. Starbucks offers health insurance to anyone who works more than 20 hours. The company respects its products, its customers, and its employees. It's listed on the *Fortune* list of 100 Best Companies to Work For.

Schultz grew up in a Brooklyn housing project. His father struggled at low-paying jobs and died with little to show for his years of hard work.

> "He was beaten down, he wasn't respected," Schultz said. "He had no health insurance, and he had no workers' compensation when he got hurt on the job." So with Starbucks, Schultz "wanted to build the kind of company that my father never got a chance to work for, in which people were respected." (*Great Entrepreneurs: Howard Schultz*)

Today, Starbucks is continuing its amazing growth. Schultz has made so much money that he bought the Seattle Supersonics basketball team for $250 million. Starbucks also gives generously to charity and works to make the world a little better. They also helped create an inspirational movie called *Akeelah and the Bee*, about a young girl and the neighborhood that worked to get her to the National Spelling Bee.

Starbucks is still making a great cup of coffee and keeping employees and customers happy. Not bad for someone from the projects who had trouble even getting a job.

Sources: *"Great Entrepreneurs: Biography: Howard Schultz, Starbucks."* MyPrimeTime 2001. Accessed June 3, 2006. www.myprimetime.com/work/ge/schultzbio/index.shtml

"Akeelah and the Bee." Starbucks. 2006. Accessed June 3, 2006. www.starbucks.com/retail/akeelah.asp

Profile Clues to Use

How did Howard Schultz develop his abilities?

_____

_____

_____

_____

_____

What are some obstacles he faced?

_____

_____

_____

_____

_____

How do you see yourself as similar or dissimilar to him?

_____

_____

_____

_____

_____

acceptance

Being true to yourself involves accepting who you are. It is one thing to understand who you are, but it is quite another thing to accept yourself, warts and all. Self-acceptance may be exceedingly difficult when friends or society tell you that you should be different from who you are. But pretending to be someone else is a sure recipe for misery.

Fully accepting who you are as a unique individual can be difficult, especially in young adulthood, because there is a lot of pressure to be like everyone else. If you would love to be in the science club but your friends convince you to join track, you probably will spend a lot of time losing races and wishing you were in the laboratory. If you can embrace who you are, however, you will find happiness a lot sooner than all those kids who are trying to copy someone else.

We all have faults and weaknesses, and it can be hard to recognize those shortcomings and accept them. However, it is important to recognize the areas in which you need to work harder or where you need to ask for help.

In recognizing these faults, it helps to be aware of the difference between acceptance and complacency. Many people may be complacent in that they may recognize their faults but don't do anything about them because they believe that is just who they are. This is complacency, and this is the behavior of underachievers. One can never improve if they are never striving to do better.

However, if someone recognizes his or her faults and then works to change or improve them, that person is being proactive. For example, being a good reader is a skill that one should develop. If poor reading skills are not addressed while you're young, it could be a life-long problem. Other areas of who you are, like being an introvert, may not have to be worked on if you do not want to work on them. It is important to be happy with who you are, while striving to be even better.

essons from tae kwon-do

One of the lessons of Tae kwon-do, the most popular of the Korean martial arts, is to be willing to go where the going may be tough and do the difficult things that are worth doing, even though they are difficult.

The Humphrey family of Phoenix, Arizona, credit this philosophy with helping them accomplish an important goal. Their mantra became: "The family that kicks together sticks together." The mother, Kim Humphrey, and two of her children have all earned black belts, martial arts' highest achievement.

As fate would have it, the decision to enroll in Tae kwon-do as a family was due, in large measure, to sibling rivalry. At the time, Kim's daughters, Lauren, who was ten, and Katie, who was eight, were enrolled in gymnastics. Katie wasn't happy that her older sister was doing better in gym class than she was, so Kim began looking for something else for her younger child to do. A friend of the family told Kim about Tae kwon-do, and Kim decided to give it a try.

Kim liked what she saw when she took her two children to class each week, so she decided to join the class herself. "I liked the tenets of Tae kwon-do and how this was something we could work on together as a family," she explains. "It got hard towards the end because there are so many requirements for a black belt, such as memorizing 20 patterns, and the final competition is nerve-wracking," explains Kim. There's a panel of judges, and your peers and their families can watch.

Kim credits their family involvement for the support they needed to keep pushing themselves forward. "If one of us didn't want to go to the practice, another family member would say, 'Come on! You have to go,'" she says.

The results have been well worth it. Even though the kids are now involved in other sports and activities, the lessons they learned in Tae kwon-do have remained with them, motivating them to perform better and persevere in other areas of life. So remember: Some of life's richest rewards are often disguised as setbacks. The Humphreys' disgruntled little sister steered the family in a whole new direction.

Overachieving

Kieffer was considered an overachiever. In high school she worked tirelessly to get straight A's. However, this goal for perfection often led her to feel overwhelmed, exhausted, and stressed. As a college student, Kieffer strove to keep these same high standards; with the heavier demands of college level work, the adjustment of living away from home for the first time, and working a part-time job, however, she could not handle it all. Kieffer pushed herself so hard that she found herself feeling sick most of the time and being too tired to go out with friends and have fun. She did not understand why many of her friends, who had the same demands that she did, seemed fine when she was so stressed.

Eventually Kieffer realized that, unlike some of her friends, she needed down-time to relax and unwind, which meant she needed fewer things to do. To cut down on her stress, Kieffer quit her job so she could focus more on school and took fewer class credits. Although Kieffer is still a perfectionist and pushes herself hard, she has learned to strive for excellence in a few areas instead of taking on too much at one time. By accepting her limitations, she has learned to compensate for her perfectionistic tendencies.

You may wish that you did not have certain weaknesses or faults, but you do. Everyone does, and that's what makes us all unique. When you are able to accept yourself, gifts and faults, strengths and weaknesses, you will have a new understanding for why you do what you do, why you feel the way you do, why you like or dislike certain things, and why you're good at certain things. Ultimately, you will understand who you are. When you understand and accept who you are, you can let your gifts and talents lead your way; this will guide you to a life of happiness and fulfillment.

The following profile illustrates how our gifts and talents can be used to impact the world in a large way.

TIGER WOODS

Mastering life

"I really do believe he was put here for a bigger reason than just to play golf."

—FORMER NBA PLAYER MICHAEL JORDAN

Tiger Woods' real name is Eldrick; his nickname was given him by his father, Earl Woods, in honor of a friend who saved Earl's life during the Vietnam War. According to the website Role Models on the Web: Tiger Woods, "Tiger started swinging a sawed off golf club in his garage at 11 months." At the age of 21, he became the youngest winner of the Masters Golf Tournament, the crowning achievement for professional golfers.

Tiger has signed a $40 million contract with Nike, and a $30 million contract with American Express. Besides wearing a green jacket every spring and selling credit cards and cars, Tiger is also passionate about education, especially after September 11, 2001. He's been quoted as saying, "I felt I hadn't done enough." About a month later, he decided to build a learning center—not to teach kids how to play golf, but to help them find an interest they are passionate about. The launch of the new Tiger Woods Learning Centers (TWLC) took place on February 10, 2006, in Anaheim, California. The goal of the TWLC is to "get students thinking about the role education plays in their futures." For more information about the TWLC, visit www.twlc.org.

Tiger seems to think that being a good role model for kids is even more important than his golf. Perhaps he thinks golf is just a vehicle for him to influence people in a positive way. Tiger has said he feels that's what life is all about.

Sources: www.rolemodel.net/tiger/tiger.htm, www.twlc.org

Profile Clues to Use

How did Tiger Woods develop his abilities?

_____

_____

_____

_____

What are some obstacles he faced?

_____

_____

_____

_____

How do you see yourself as similar or dissimilar to him?

_____

_____

_____

_____

t hink globally

Tiger Woods is a leader not only in golf but in the field of education. He represents our multicultural world, coming from an ethnic background of African, Thai, Chinese, Native American, and European.

We live in a complicated world, and the problems we see today are so huge that it takes everyone doing his or her part to make a difference. Think about this:*

---

*Statistics are according to the humanitarian organization World Vision, www.worldvision.org/.

- More than half the world's population—that's 3.8 billion people—survives on less than $2 a day.
- Almost 11 million young children die every year, most from preventable diseases.
- A child who is 5 years old or younger dies every 20 seconds from a preventable water-related disease.
- More than 15 million children around the world have lost one or both parents to HIV/AIDS; 6,000 children are orphaned by AIDS every day.
- Nearly 20 percent of the adult world is illiterate.

The problems are gigantic; if we work together and combine our gifts and talents, however, we can chip away at the chaos.

Gifts and talents don't have to be used only to benefit you. They can be given away and used to make a difference in the world. Imagine for a moment that I handed you a beautifully wrapped gift and asked you to deliver it to a particular person tomorrow. And as long as you delivered the gift, you'd get to keep one just like it for yourself. Next week, I see you and you're still holding the gift. "It's so perfect," you tell me. "I decided to keep it for myself." Sounds ridiculous, doesn't it? But this is often what we do with the gifts and talents we have. We keep them to ourselves and never share them with those who would benefit from them.

act locally

Right now, right where you are, strive to do your very best, even in the so-called little things. Those who prove themselves capable of doing little things can be given greater responsibilities. Becoming excellent in many things opens the door to more opportunities. If your teacher sends you on an errand to the school office, do it to the best of your ability. If your coach asks you to run laps, do it to the best of your ability. If you're asked to wash the dishes, do it to the best of your ability. Look around you at home, at school, and in your community, and do something to help someone.

become aware

An article in *Newsweek* magazine dated June 12, 2006, titled, "How Long Will America Lead?" reveals why Americans are losing ground as a leading force in the workplace. U. S. students are beginning to fall behind their global counterparts in test scores and in job power.

"Americans," the reporter, Fareed Zakaria, writes, "don't quite realize how fast the rest of the world is catching up. No worker from a rich country [like the United States] can equal the energy of someone trying to move out of poverty." Students from places like China and Romania are hungry to succeed.

In response to this growing education crisis, many high schools are "trying to provide the best work force in the world. Not in the country—in the world." Schools are creating freshmen success programs and ninth-grade academies to help students work on weak subject areas and to help them gain life skills. LifeBound, the publisher of this book, is at the forefront of this movement by providing top-notch resources for educators and students.

These innovative schools also offer career-themed "schools within a school" that emphasize subjects like engineering, science, or business. For example, Chad Lewis, a high school student in North Carolina, is taking classes in **hydraulics** and electrical systems so that he can learn to work on diesel engines. This enables him to earn up to two years of college credits before he graduates, the equivalent of an associate's college degree. What it also means, says his math teacher, is that "he'll be making more money than I will."

Hydraulics *n.* a branch of science that deals with practical applications (as the transmission of energy or the effects of flow) of liquid (as water) in motion

the future is in your hands

The bottom line is that no one can do the work for you. Only you can discover your gifts and figure out the best way for you to use them. Only you can decide what really works in your life and what doesn't. You are the one responsible for your choices. Keep working on the tasks and projects discussed in this book that help you find your gifts and talents. You might even consider putting it aside for a year, re-doing the exercises, and comparing your responses from both years. You'll be amazed at how far you can go in just one year if you're willing to focus on exploring what you're about. As we've tried to convey in this book, you can use your gifts and talents to enrich yourself as well as the lives of others. We hope this book has encouraged you to explore your gifts and talents and to use them wisely.

SELF-DISCOVERY ACTIVITY

We want to hear from you!

Please visit our website (www.lifebound.com) and send in your stories about how you found and developed your gifts or talents, or send us your questions. Also, please complete the following questionnaire and send it in.

LifeBound Reviewer Questionnaire

Please spend a few moments giving us your feedback on this book and send it to contact@lifebound.com. Thank you!

Your Name: _____

Your School or relationship to LifeBound: _____

Phone: _____ Email: _____

Address: _____

Your age or the grade you teach: _____

What was your impression of this book's content? _____

_____

What is missing or neglected? _____

_____

Did this book benefit you and/or your students?   ◯ Yes   ◯ No

Why? _____

_____

Would you like to review other manuscripts that LifeBound is working on?

◯ Yes   ◯ No

Would your students review the manuscript?   ◯ Yes   ◯ No

What, if anything else, should have been included in the appendices? ___

_____

How do you rate the book overall?   Low   1 2 3 4 5 6 7 8 9 10   High

Would you like to subscribe to our newsletter?   ◯ Yes   ◯ No

Additional thoughts or comments: _____

_____

_____

For information about LifeBound's books and curriculum, visit our website at www.lifebound.com or contact the author, Carol Carter, at contact@lifebound.com. Or you can write to us at

LifeBound, LLC
1530 High Street
Denver, CO 80218

Tel. 303.327.5688 (in Colorado)

Fax 303.327.5684

Toll free 1.877.737.8510 (outside Colorado)

your journal

Each of the following journal pages has a quote or a question for you to think about. Use the quotes and related questions to guide your writing. Journaling allows you to see how your thoughts grow and change over time. You will also learn more about yourself as you continue in your journaling. Write about your thoughts, your daily life, your dreams for the future, or anything else you deem worthy.

Hide not your talents, they for use were made.
What's a sun-dial in the shade?

—BENJAMIN FRANKLIN

What is one particular profile story in the book that stood out for you, and why?

> The highest reward for man's toil is not what he gets for it,
> but what he becomes by it.
>
> —JOHN RUSKIN

How might your abilities shape who you are?

> *They are able because they think they are able.*
>
> —VIRGIL

What activity or experience makes you feel capable and joyful?

> I don't know the key to success, but the key to failure is trying to please everybody.
>
> —BILL COSBY

What are some things you wish people knew about you?

> Everyone must row with the oars he has.
>
> —ENGLISH PROVERB

Of the things that you are good at, write about two or three that you think have real potential.

_____

_____

_____

_____

_____

_____

_____

_____

_____

_____

_____

_____

_____

_____

_____

_____

_____

_____

_____

_____

_____

_____

_____

_____

> Success is getting what you want; happiness is wanting what you get.
>
> —DALE CARNEGIE

What does a happy, fulfilled life look like?

Use what talents you possess: The woods would be very silent if no birds sang there except those that sang best.

—HENRY VAN DYKE

Define gifted *in your own words.*

_____

_____

_____

_____

_____

_____

_____

_____

_____

_____

_____

_____

_____

_____

_____

_____

_____

_____

_____

_____

_____

_____

_____

_____

_____

_____

> *There is a great distance between said and done.*
>
> —PUERTO RICAN PROVERB

Write about the last time you were satisfied with a job you had done. What did the job involve?

> *Imagination is more important than knowledge.*
>
> —ALBERT EINSTEIN

What would you like to see come out of the abilities you have?

> Sometimes it is more important to discover what one cannot do than what one can do.
>
> —LIN YUTANG

Why might this be true?

> *Natural abilities are like natural plants that need pruning by study.*
>
> —FRANCIS BACON

In what ways can you try to improve your life?

> Toil to make yourself remarkable by some talent or other.
>
> —SENECA

What roles do practice and work play in developing talent?

> Life is like a ten-speed bike. Most of us have gears we never use.
>
> —CHARLES SCHULZ

In what activities (school, clubs, hobbies, etc.) do you think you could take part as a way of discovering your own gifts and talents?

> You are responsible for the talent that has been entrusted to you.
>
> —HENRI-FRÉDÉRIC AMIEL

Do you think that your set of talents are set in stone, or do you think that they can evolve?

> *Talent is like electricity—we do not understand electricity. We use it.*
>
> —MAYA ANGELOU

Can you think of any activities that you are already involved in that, if pursued, might reveal a talent?

> It is not enough to have a good mind. The main thing is to use it well.
>
> —RENÉ DESCARTES

Brainstorm about some of your gifts and talents. What career paths might be related to those things?

We are always more anxious to be distinguished for a talent which we do not possess, than to be praised for the fifteen which we do possess.

—MARK TWAIN

If you had fifteen minutes of fame, what would you like it to be for?

> If you have a talent, use it in every which way possible. Don't hoard it. Don't dole it out like a miser. Spend it lavishly like a millionaire intent on going broke.
>
> —BRENDAN FRANCIS

What are some ways that you can use your abilities to help someone else?

> The happiness of a man in this life depends not on the absence but the mastery of his passions.
>
> —ALFRED LORD TENNYSON

What can you do right now to start realizing your dreams?

resources

Lifebound Resources

LifeBound offers the following products and services:

- Books and curriculum
- Tutoring
- Individual student or parent coaching
- Faculty development seminars
- Training and certification to become a LifeBound coach
- Career coaching
- Free monthly e-letter

For more information, contact the LifeBound office toll free at 1.877.737.8510 or visit us online at www.lifebound.com.

General Resources

Books

People Smarts for Teenagers: Becoming Emotionally Intelligent, by Carol Carter (Denver: Lifebound, 2005).

Keys to Effective Learning: Developing Powerful Habits of Mind (4th ed.), by Carol Carter, Joyce Bishop and Sarah Lyman Kravits (Upper Saddle River, NJ: Pearson/Prentice Hall, 2005).

Student/Educator Websites

www.lifebound.com
www.ntatutor.org
www.teencentral.net/
www.teenhelp.org/
http://teenshealth.org/teen/

Mentoring Websites

www.mentoring.org/
http://icouldbe.org/
Peer Mentoring: www.chumz.net/
Big Brothers, Big Sisters: www.bbbsa.org/

Other Success Books by Carol Carter

The following books are available through Prentice Hall Publishers.
Visit www.prenhall.com (search by keywords "keys to").

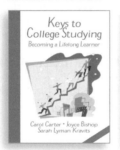

The following books are available through LifeBound. Visit www.lifebound.com.

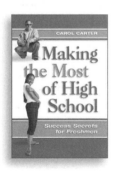
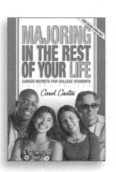

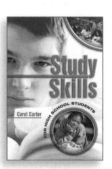

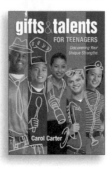

College and Career Planning

Books

Majoring in the Rest of Your Life: Career Secrets for College Students (4th ed.), by Carol Carter (Denver: LifeBound, 2005).

Careermap: Deciding What You Want, Getting It, and Keeping It, by Neil M. Yeager (Somerset, NJ: John Wiley & Sons, 1988).

Websites

www.lifebound.com

http://geostudies.com/

http://collegeboard.com/

www.petersons.com/

Professional Development for Educators

Now, Discover Your Strengths, by Marcus Buckingham and Donald Clifton (London: Simon & Schuster, 2001).

The World Is Flat, by Thomas L. Friedman (New York: Farrar, Straus and Giroux, 2005).

On Being a Teacher, by Jonathan Kozol (New York: Continuum, 1981).

Shame of the Nation, by Jonathan Kozol (New York: Crown, 2005).

LifeBound Coaching

Carol Carter offers training and certification to become a LifeBound coach in partnership with the National Tutoring Association (NTA) at www.ntatutor.org.

Carol Carter also offers faculty and professional development training. Contact the LifeBound office toll free at 1.877.737.8510 or visit us online at www.lifebound.com or write:

LifeBound	Tel. 303.327.5688
1530 High Street	Fax 303.327.5684
Denver, CO 80218	Email caroljcarter@lifebound.com

We look forward to hearing from you!